Engendering Modernity

ENGENDERING MODERNITY

Feminism, Social Theory and Social Change

Barbara L. Marshall

Polity Press

Copyright © Barbara L. Marshall 1994

The right of Barbara L. Marshall to be identified as author of this work has been asserted in accordance with the Copyright, Designs and Patents Act 1988.

First published in 1994 by Polity Press in association with Blackwell Publishers

Editorial office:
Polity Press
65 Bridge Street
Cambridge CB2 1UR, UK

Marketing and production:
Blackwell Publishers
108 Cowley Road
Oxford OX4 1JF, UK

ISBN 0 7456 0927 9
ISBN 0 7456 0928 7 (pbk)

British Library Cataloguing-in-Publication Data
A CIP catalogue record for this book is available from the British Library.

Typeset in 12 on 13 pt Garamond by Photoprint, Torquay.
Printed in Great Britain by T.J. Press, Padstow, Cornwall

This book is printed on acid-free paper.

Contents

For my mother, Maeve Marshall

Acknowledgements

This book has taken shape over a long period of time, during which many teachers, colleagues and students assisted me in developing my analysis. In particular I wish to thank Graham Lowe, Harvey Krahn, Derek Sayer, Susan Jackel, Marg Hobbs, Joan Sangster, Sedef Arat-Koç, Susan Lang, Robyn Diner, David Brown and Marie Carlson for stimulating many of the ideas developed here. My greatest intellectual debt is to Ray Morrow, who as both teacher and friend has always pushed me to think things through and, while we have not always agreed on the answers, has suggested many of the questions that I have tackled.

I am grateful to the Social Sciences and Humanities Research Council of Canada for financial support in the form of a doctoral fellowship, as well as to Trent University for a Research Fellowship and a grant from the Sub-committee on Research in the Arts.

Friends and family deserve much of the credit for seeing this book through to fruition. Special thanks to Frances Adams, for always being there, and to Judy Pinto, for keeping my life organized. Love and thanks go especially to my husband, Yiannis Kiparissis, who has borne more than his fair share of both domestic labour and the frustrations of writer's block. Our daughter Lucy, born during the preparation of the manuscript, has made it all worthwhile.

Finally, the people at Polity Press have been a delight to work with, from start to finish.

Permission to use previously published material was generously granted as follows:

Some of the material in Chapter 3 was published in my 'Critical Theory and Feminist Theory', *Canadian Review of Sociology and Anthropology*, 25 (2), 1988, and is used here by permission of that journal.

An earlier version of Chapter 4 was previously published as 'Reproducing the Gendered Subject', in *Current Perspectives in Social Theory*, 11 (1991), and is used here by permission of JAI Press.

Introduction

This is a book about theory, written at a time when the very practice of theory has become increasingly suspect. I write as a feminist, and as a sociologist, who has been caught up in the debates about the status and purpose of theory, and who has had to confront some of the resulting questions about theory in both my teaching and my research. The practice of theory has been deeply affected by the debates about modernity versus postmodernity, and the attendant questions of the possibility of social theory which can foster human autonomy and emancipation. The assertions by certain theorists, such as Baudrillard, Derrida, Foucault, Lyotard and Rorty, that such theoretical aspirations are tied irredeemably to the now passé modern *épistème*, suggest that theory as an emancipatory project is indeed at an end. My basic premise is that these assertions are far from neutral. I see them as emanating from the same position of false universalism as that of the theoretical tradition they criticize. In other words, they express, as Christine Di Stephano puts it, the 'claims and needs of a constituency (white, privileged men of the industrialized West) that has already had an Enlightenment for itself and that is now ready and willing to subject that legacy to critical scrutiny' (1990: 75). Just as feminist historians and social theorists begin to reconstruct the ambivalent relationship of women to modernity, and to breathe new life into its emancipatory project, this very project is deemed bankrupt. I want to argue that, flawed as it is, the modern project still contains considerable potential to ground an emancipatory practice, and that some recent feminist theory is paradigmatic of how such a project might be reconstructed – or engendered.

I first used the term 'engender', in the manner in which I use it here, several years ago as I was working on a conference paper on women and the welfare state. I was struggling for a term which recognized the crucial role gender played in the initial construction of the welfare state, and which captured the active way in which gender is continually embedded in the operation of, and our experience of, welfare states today. I chose the term engendering both for its dictionary meaning of 'engender' – to enable or bring about – and for etymological reasons. The prefix 'en-' is commonly used to make a transitive verb out of a noun, as in 'endear' or 'encircle'. Thus it is in this dual sense that I want to speak of engendering modernity. I want to draw attention to the restructuring of gender relations as a fundamental characteristic of modernity, and to nurture a feminist vision of the emancipatory potential of social theory as a modern project.

To do this requires some major rethinking of the basic analytical categories of social theory, categories such as 'the individual', 'society', 'class', 'citizenship'. The experience of women has always been peripheral to the construction of these categories, and as this experience is reclaimed and inserted into the heart of social theory, the inadequacy of these categories, as traditionally conceived, becomes painfully apparent. Singled out for particular critique is the relationship between the individual and society as this has been understood in both classical and contemporary theories of modernity. The 'sociological individual', while ostensibly the universal subject of modernity, obscures a deeply gendered analysis of social life. Such a conception of the individual is premised upon a set of dualistic categories, such as public versus private, economy versus family, universal versus particular, which are constructed on the experience of Western, white, heterosexual males, and which have been overly abstracted and reified in social theory. As we begin to deconstruct these dualisms to better account for wider experiences of social life, the potential for theorizing the individual–society relationship in new ways arises. New questions around the subject and political agency, and the emergence of distinctively modern contexts for identity formation rise to the top of the theoretical agenda. The central aim of this book, then, is to undertake the dual tasks of providing a revised account of modernity – one which includes the experience of women – and of considering what sort of a theoretical framework might be built on this revised account.

But do we need more theory? More specifically, do we need to take another stab at reconstructing 'malestream' theory? Some feminists view the sort of theoretical reconstruction I am proposing in a critical light. For example, as Stanley and Wise (1990: 43) characterize it, its aim is 'to clean up theoretical inadequacies *at the level of theory*, then to turn to small, carefully presented snippets of life to exemplify the success of the theoretical project'. The concern here, they charge, is 'with marking out a privileged role for feminist researchers in the production of "Theory" (with a decidedly capital T) as a transcendent and so privileged account of the realities of other women's lives'. Obviously, I view this project differently. I think it is important to understand theory, even (or perhaps, especially) non-feminist theory. The traditions of Western intellectual thought have shaped the way in which we see ourselves, and the way in which we construct and see 'others'. It is only by coming to terms with the way in which these theoretical traditions have been constructed to fracture our vision that we can begin to see things anew. As Lerner (1986: 13) suggests, the insight that 'men are not the centre of the world, but men and women are. . .will transform consciousness as decisively as did Copernicus's discovery that the earth is not the centre of the universe'. This transformation has continued as women of colour, unchilded women, poor women, lesbians and non-Western women, speaking from their experience, challenge the narrowness of the subject of earlier versions of feminist theories. These challenges have enriched and deepened our analytical perspectives. Yet a transcendental dimension is integral to the development of a critical social theory – direct experience does not exhaust the understanding of forces which shape our lives. An articulation of everyday experience to historically situated socio-economic and cultural formations is necessary. To continue with the Copernican analogy, social theory can help make sense of and *transform* our experience, 'just as our experience of the sun's sinking below the horizon has been transformed by our knowledge that the world turns and that our location in the world turns away from the sun – even though from where we are it seems to sink' (D. Smith, 1987: 89).

The difference between theory as *theory*, which seeks explanation, prediction and/or understanding of a phenomenon, and theory as *critique*, which calls forth action in the world, is crucial. Theory as critique has a long theoretical pedigree,[1] and those who endorse the project of critical theory today continue to find rich insights in Marx. As Fraser (1989: 113) suggests, Marx's conceptualization of critical theory as 'the self clarification of the struggles and wishes of the age' has yet to be surpassed. Critical theory, in its late twentieth-century manifestations, has gone far beyond Marx's critique of capitalism to attempt to clarify struggles which reach far beyond the realm of production. While the term 'critical theory' is most closely associated with the tradition of the Frankfurt Institute for Social Research, and with Jürgen Habermas, the best-known 'heir' of that tradition, I will use it to refer to a broader range of theories which embody some of the ideals of the Frankfurt tradition as described by Guess (1981: 2): 'A critical theory. . .is a reflective theory which gives agents a kind of knowledge inherently productive of enlightenment and emancipation.' Thus conceived, critical theory is, with all its problems, 'the best of what is left of the Left' (Poster, 1989: 3).

My aim is not so much to argue for the utility of critical theory for feminism – I believe that feminists have been *doing* critical theory better than many self-proclaimed critical theorists for a long time – as to argue for the centrality of feminist theory for the development of critical social theory. Feminist theories have shared the ambivalent relationship of critical theory to the modernist tradition, questioning the ontology of labour central to Marxism yet unwilling to abandon its emancipatory project, and eschewing the faith in science represented by positivism in favour of multiple and reflective methodological strategies grounded in a critical knowledge-interest. However, I prefer the term critical feminist theory to socialist feminist theory, not so much to identify it with any particular stream of 'malestream' critical theory, but to get away from the association of socialist feminist theories with productivist models of society, which tend to make 'feminist' a qualifier of 'socialist'. A truly critical theory is indeed socialist, but it is equally feminist and anti-racist. It is committed to the critique of all forms of domination and distortion.

One of my motivations for writing this book has been my concern with the extent to which some of the most exciting developments in theoretical thinking have occurred in relative isolation from one another (due, in no small part, to the continued marginalization of feminism in the academy), and with the tendency to recycle this isolation in the manner in which we teach theory to our students. This concern has influenced the selection of theories and concepts that frame my analysis. I have attempted to provide some openings for readers without extensive grounding in the feminist literature to see the convergence of feminist critiques with problems in social theory more generally, but have tried to avoid simply presenting a 'survey' of that literature. Thus, what follows is just one way of mapping the theoretical terrain. I have focused on some theories to the neglect of others, and have made some broad generalizations from different national contexts. I have tried to identify some of the significant points of intersection between different theoretical traditions, which means that others are ignored or underdeveloped. Those more swayed than I by the postmodern turn in theory will no doubt find my analysis lacking. Similarly, given my concern to recount a particular history of 'received' theory in the social sciences, I have not given extensive coverage of some of the more recent advances in, for example, feminist philosophy and psycho-analysis.[2] In spite of these limitations, I hope what follows will serve as a useful review and reconstruction of some important debates, while at the same time pushing those who embrace the goals of a critical social theory to become more explicitly feminist.

Chapter 1 will take modernity, and the relationship between modernity and capitalism, as the central problematic of classical social theory. I will look at how women have figured as a strategic absence in both classical and contemporary debates, resulting in a conception of the individual, and the individual–society relation-ship, which has profound implications for the manner in which we understand gender inequalities. Chapter 2 will re-examine the gendered division of labour as a fundamental concept in 'explaining' gender differences – in both feminist and non-feminist theories. Here, I will argue that prevailing theories of the division of labour have (a) rested on an overly narrow conception of labour, (b) neglected the degree to which gender divisions shape both the material and ideological forms that the social division of labour takes, and (c) reified both the public–private dualism and its coincidence with a gendered division of labour. Building on this critique, I will review, in chapter 3, the genesis of socialist feminist theory in terms of a 'reproduction problematic'. After examining the manner in which feminist theory has challenged the Marxist conception of social reproduction, I will look at some current impasses in socialist feminist theory and suggest how we might begin to move beyond them. Chapter 4 takes the theorization of subjectivity as a central problematic for a critical social theory, and suggests that feminism has much to contribute to this project. Against both essentialist theories of gendered subjects and the poststructuralist dissolution of the subject, I will focus on the multiple and often contradictory nature of subjectivity, and on the active construction of gendered identities in terms of historically available modes of interpretation. Chapter 5 focuses on the role of the state and political discourse in the regulation of gendered identities, and looks at theories which suggest the possibility of emergent public spaces which might promote the contestation of identities. Finally, in chapter 6, I will suggest that social science cannot fully understand 'modernity' (nor, for that matter, postmodernity) until it comes to terms with the one-sided story it has constructed, and that the inherently political nature of feminist theory has the potential to revitalize the project of a critical social theory.

1
Gender and Modernity: Classical Issues, Contemporary Debates

1.1 Modernity and Social Theory: The Classical Connection

The connection between sociology and modernity is well rehearsed in the 'history of theory' texts.[1] While 'modernization' may be broadly understood as the transition from 'simple', homogenous societies to 'complex', highly differentiated ones, with the attendant questions about social order and social change, the discourse of 'modernity' includes the larger philosophical questions, dating back to the Enlightenment, surrounding rationalization as the underpinning of both modernization and the interpretations of progress in Western social and political thought.

Against the backdrop of the Enlightenment, modernity is associated with the release of the individual from the bonds of tradition, with the progressive differentiation of society, with the emergence of civil society, with political equality, with innovation and change. All of these accomplishments are associated with capitalism, industrialism, secularization, urbanization and rationalization. The changes associated with the advent of modernity were integral to the development of social theory.

Modern social and political theory took root in the Enlightenment abandonment of traditional religious authorities for a belief in human reason and progress. In sharp contrast to theological world views, Enlightenment thought promoted the radical view that the human condition could be understood scientifically, and that this understanding would promote progress and human emancipation. But, lest we get carried away with a celebration of modernity's gains, remember that it is the 'dark side' of modernity that has provided most of the traditional subject matter for sociological theory. The major works by classical sociological theorists such as Comte, Marx, Durkheim, Weber and Simmel were centrally concerned with the reconstruction of order out of the decline of traditional authority, and sought to apply reason to the problem of integration given the change from simple to complex, traditional to modern, homogeneity to heterogeneity that they witnessed with the coming of a new industrial order. The growing social division of labour was a vital concern of classical theory, as was the shifting relationship between the individual and society. The dissolution of traditional communal bonds was perceived as a potential threat to interpersonal relations and social integration. Classical social theory was born out of a sense of social crisis. As Turner (1992: 185) notes, the transition from Gemeinschaft to Gesellschaft, which defined the terrain of the classical project, stocked the conceptual toolkit that is still standard issue for social theorists — alienation, anomie, rationalization, disenchantment. The truth or falsity of the story of the birth of the modern is not the issue — what is significant is the self-understanding of the discipline in these terms: 'In this respect we can analyse sociology as a primarily nostalgic discourse which recounts how authentic communities were destroyed by the ineluctable advance of industrial capitalism across urban space, leaving behind it the debris of egoistic individualism, other-directed personalities, anomic cultures and homeless minds' (Turner, 1992: 185).

Less well rehearsed in the theory textbooks is a feminist understanding of the 'project of modernity'.[2] The erasure of gender in the classical project is significant on two counts. First, it raises questions about the nostalgic story that modern social theory was born out of social upheaval — and is integral to the political and intellectual current of the post-Enlightenment. As Kandal (1988: 4) notes, 'classical sociological theory originated in the same historical epoch as the long swell of modern feminism, flowing in pulses and lulls roughly from the eighteenth century to the present'.

Writings by feminists such as Mary Wollstonecraft and Harriet Martineau, as well as feminist political movements which were in full swing by the end of the nineteenth century, were virtually ignored by classical social theorists. But perhaps more importantly, the exclusion of women from the heart of the classical project has resulted in a skewed picture of social life, of the very subject matter of sociology. The changes associated with modernity — such as the separation of the family from wider kinship groups, the separation of the household and economy (which entailed the radical transformation of both), and the emergence of the modern state — are all *gendered* processes. The roles which emerged alongside the differentiation of the economy and the state from the household — worker, citizen — were (are) *gendered* roles. As it was theoretically understood in the classical tradition, the social differentiation so central to sociological accounts of modernity was based on male experience. For example, both civil society and the state (the separation of these standing as a hallmark of modernity) were defined in terms of their distinction from the family. Treated as a central organizing principle in the old order, kinship as conceived of in modernity makes women and children disappear from the public world. The purpose of the family, and woman within it, becomes, depending on the theorist, a moral regulator of, a reproducer of, or a haven for, the male individual.

The distinction between the 'public' and the 'private' is central to theories of modernity. Classical sociological theory developed, in part, as a response to and corrective of classical liberal theory. In both liberalism and in classical sociological theory, the relationship between public and private is basic to the theorization of the individual–society relationship. While in liberal theory the individual is conceived of as pre-existent to society, the starting point for classical sociological theory is the reverse of this ontological equation. That is, the individual is theorized as *social* — as constituted only within society. As classical sociological theory developed, it inverted the asociality of the individual as constructed in liberalism, and it is within the general problematic of the individual–society relationship that we can locate the public–private division. The social differentiation of modern societies creates modern individuals. This is the underpinning of the discipline. Given this, the sociological inversion of the individual–

society relationship of liberalism should have been able to embrace the theorization of public and private spheres as both wholly social, yet it was not successful in this respect (Yeatman, 1986). To elaborate, I will first review briefly the liberal formulation of the individual–society relationship and the separation of public and private spheres, then outline the attempts of sociological theory to reconstruct this relationship. As we shall see, the result has largely been to set up a public–private dualism which is easily conflated with the dualism of male–female, and which constructs a sociological individual whose ostensibly universal cloak hides an implicitly gendered constitution.

For liberalism, the line is drawn between public and private to delineate the role of the state. Classical liberalism was founded on the doctrine of individual freedom, 'whether defined as freedom from coercion, as moral self-determination, or as the right to individual happiness' (Seidman, 1983: 15). Defence of these basic freedoms necessarily required clear limits on their restriction by the state. Individual freedoms are translated into individual 'rights', which the state is bound to administrate and uphold. The most fundamental right is the right to privacy and the public becomes necessary to secure the private – chiefly private property and the privacy of interpersonal associations. The classic distinction between public and private, then, is that between the public world of politics, and the private world of economic and familial relationships. Locke's statement that 'every Man has a Property in his own Person' lays the basis for the idea that freedom equals the right to enter a contract regarding that property (Pateman, 1988: 13). 'Civil society' straddles the two realms of public and private as the locus of the contract, the state being the impartial (public) arbitrator of contracts between freely-acting (private) individuals. Liberal economic theory further presupposes 'a distinction between the public, "economic" world of the market and the private "non-economic" sphere of the home' (Jaggar, 1983: 144). There is a sharp distinction within the liberal tradition, then, between political philosophy and economic theory, each orientated to a particular set of questions, but similarly deriving their conception of the social, and hence the public and the private, from the level of the individual. There is no question that the individual of liberalism was male; women were excluded from the public in both its political and economic senses, being subsumed under the authority of their husbands and/or fathers. They could not own property or sign contracts in their own right, neither was the bulk of their labour undertaken in terms of a labour contract. The marriage contract provided their only articulation as individuals to the public realm. Liberalism is thus not only premised upon the distinction between public and private, but separates out the domestic, and hence women, as particularly private.

The distinction between the state (public) and the family (private) was made most clearly by Locke in *Two Treatises of Government* (1689) in terms of a distinction between political and paternal authority: 'the Power of a Magistrate over a Subject, may be distinguished from that of a Father over his Children, a Master over his Servant, a Husband over his Wife, and a Lord over his Slave. . . .But these two Powers, Political and Paternal, are so perfectly distinct and separate; are built upon so different Foundations and given to so different Ends' (cited in Nicholson, 1986: 152). The privatization of the family, and the legitimation of patriarchal authority in the private sphere, derive from the ontological priority granted to the individual in liberal theory. Thus, in classical liberal theory, the positioning of the individual as prior to and partially outside of society permitted the exclusion of women from society.

Marx developed his theory in sharp opposition to liberalism, seeing politics and economics as intimately related. For Marx, the distinction between public and private in liberal political philosophy is largely illusory, and he rejects 'the conception of anything as private, as standing outside society or as prior to it, as unrelated to other people and of no concern to them, or as resting on the rights and claims of single persons' (Kamenka, 1983: 274). The state is no impartial arbitrator, but an instrument of that class which controls the means of production. Politics becomes economic, and economics political. But what of the familial?

For Marx, abandoning Hegel's conception of the distinction between family, civil society and state, civil society 'is the true source and theatre of all history. . . .Civil society embraces the whole material intercourse of individuals within a definite stage of the development of productive forces. It embraces the whole commercial and industrial life of a given stage and, insofar, transcends the State and the nation' (Marx and Engels, 1845–6/ 1970: 57). Placing this conception of civil society into his broader theoretical framework, Marx offers the following account of the relationship between spheres: 'Assume a particular state of development in the productive forces of man and you will get a particular form of commerce and consumption. Assume particular stages of development in production, commerce and consumption and you will have a corresponding social constitution, a correspond- ing organization of the family, of orders or of classes, in a word, a corresponding civil society' (Marx, 1847/1963: 180). Yet he is fairly clear that this is an historically emergent relationship, as 'civil society as such only develops with the bourgeoisie' (Marx and Engels, 1845–6/1970: 57). Civil society has, 'as its basis and premises', the family. It is in the family, and the 'separation of society into families opposed to one another' that we find the roots of the division of labour, property relations, and the contradictory relationship between individual and society:

> The more deeply we go back into history, the more does the individual, and hence also the producing individual, appear as dependent, as belonging to a greater whole: in a still quite natural way in the family and in the family expanded into the clan. . . .Only in the eighteenth century, in 'civil society', do the various forms of social connectedness confront the individual as a mere means towards his private purposes, as external necessity (Marx, 1973: 84).

Civil society, then, is based in the contradiction of individual and society, and it is out of this contradiction that the state emerges: 'divorced from the real interests of individual and community, and at the same time as an illusory communal life, always based, however, on the real ties existing in every family and tribal conglomeration' (Marx and Engels, 1845–6/1970: 53). It is the historical domination of relations of exchange over social relation- ships which 'has reduced the family relation to a mere money relation' (Marx and Engels, 1848/1948: 11). Marx appears to retain here an idealized notion of family relationships – one which has only been tainted by capitalist economic relationships.

Nicholson (1986) notes a contradiction within Marx's formulation. That is, Marx recognized the historical and contingent nature of the capitalist mode of production, but retreated into a philosophical anthropology of kinship. By analytically subordinating the family to civil society and economic imperatives, 'Marx denies the specific logic of the family' (Mills, 1987: 81). As a result, classical Marxism cannot theorize the specificity of the domestic sphere, nor the sexual or psychodynamic politics within it.

Marxist theory does take a normative stance on the exclusion of women from public life, focusing on the private character of their labour. Women's oppression becomes associated with the emergence of private property. Private property, essential to the liberal conception of individual freedoms, illustrates for Marx a central contradiction of capitalism – that is, the private control of socially produced goods. The experience of work is placed not in a network of atomistic individual relationships, but in a network of *social* relationships. In this way, the division between public and domestic as it accompanied the emergence of private property is central to Engels' views (1884/1972: 137) on the oppression of women: 'Household management lost its public character. It no longer concerned society. It became a private service; the wife became the head servant excluded from all participation in social production.' As Dorothy Smith (1985: 5) notes, Engels oversimplifies, but nonetheless draws attention to an important distinction between the liberal and Marxist conceptions of women's labour within the public–private dualism: 'He did not see the division of labour simply as a distribution of work in work roles. Rather he saw the work process as articulated to social relations which defined its relation to others and hence defined how the doer of that work was related in society.'

Durkheim's study of the division of labour (1893/1933) also constituted a critical attack on the utilitarian individualism of classical liberal political economy. Where for the latter collective identity was derived from order imposed by the state on individuals in civil society, Durkheim differentiated between 'individuation' and 'individualism'. He set out to explain the paradox that the individual, while becoming more autonomous, also becomes more closely dependent on society. The answer, of course, lay in his analysis of the division of labour. As he summarized it:

> The division of labour appears to us otherwise than it does to the economists. For them, it essentially consists in greater production. For us, this greater productivity is only a. . .repercussion of the phenomenon. If we specialize, it is not to produce more, but it is to enable us to live in new conditions of existence that have been made for us (Durkheim, 1893/1933: 275)

As the division of labour expands and mechanical solidarity declines, the individual no longer shares the same characteristics as all other individuals in society — the individual is more and more a particular, differentiated personality. At the same time that the individual becomes particularized via the division of labour, there is increasing awareness of the common properties which each particular individual shares with the rest of humanity. It is thus the *generalized* individual which is united through 'moral individualism', the content of the 'conscience collective'. It is clear throughout Durkheim's writings that the 'generalized individual' who provided the basis for social solidarity was male. For Durkheim, 'society' itself is 'a code word for the interests and needs of men as opposed to those of women' (Sydie, 1987: 46). While the structure of domestic life was indeed social, and the nurturing of individual personality essential to the individualism that underpinned the division of labour, it was only the *male* who became individuated outside the family, and thus it was males, and male activity, that constituted the public sphere of 'society'. Durkheim thus 'solves' the individual–society paradox of modernity at the expense of women's individuation, confining them to the private, or pre-social realm of the domestic sphere. In a striking departure from his insistence on *sociological* explanation, he asserts that while men are 'almost entirely the product of society', women remain 'to a far greater extent the product of nature' (Durkheim, 1897/1951: 385). While he expects that women will eventually become more social, it will be in such a way as to exacerbate their fundamental differences from men.

Key elements of Durkheim's formulation — most notably the construction of the public sphere upon the generalized (male) individual, and the negation of women's individuality by their consignment to privacy — have retained a tenacious hold in social theory. As in Marxism, the domestic is treated as an element incorporated into 'modern' society in its transition from previous social formations, and thus retains a distinctly pre-social tenor. Where Durkheim and Marx differ most sharply on the family is in the emphasis on its social versus economic character in relation to the public sphere. It is the difference between a material and a moral interpretation of modernity.

A number of later theories of modernity have drawn extensively on Weber's writings on rationality as a means to understanding 'the place of the individual in the modern world' (Whimster and Lash, 1987: 1). Against the reification of the 'social' or the 'economic' as independent entities, Weber returns to the individual as actor. Significant here is the introduction of individual subjectivity as the conduit through which collective influences act.

Rationality, specifically instrumental rationality, is the 'hallmark of modernity' (Benjamin, 1988: 184). In accordance with most of the classical project, Weber's conception of history was largely built around the transition from traditional, personal forms of domination and authority to impersonal, economic forms. While Marx focused on the tyranny of the market, the ascendance of legal–rational authority was, for Weber, the defining characteristic of modernity. As Sydie (1987: 181) notes, women were 'dealt out' of the structure of authority and power from the beginning, through a thorough naturalization of the mother–child relationship and the rule of the father in the family. In Weber's account of capitalist development, the spread of bureaucracy and the state illustrated the growth of the 'iron cage' of a totally administered society, where impersonal relationships replace personal relationships, and human action is geared to activities of exchange and control. Jeffrey Alexander (1987: 197) summarized Weber's argument thus:

> rationalization results not only in increased autonomy but in the spread of impersonal domination through every sphere of life. The increased capacity for this-worldly calculation sustains individuation, it is true. But it simultaneously facilitates subjection and domination. Weber invented the concept of rationalization to explain the seemingly irreconcilable qualities of the twentieth century.

The 'disenchantment of the world' culminates in the retreat of 'the ultimate and most sublime values' from public life 'either into the transcendental realm of mystic life or into the brotherliness of direct and personal human relations' (Weber, 1946: 155). We are thus 'placed into various life-spheres, each of which is governed by different laws' (p. 123). The rational, calculating sphere of bureaucratic capitalism dominated; retreat into the 'gentler' spheres of emotion and religion was for those who couldn't 'bear the fate of the times like a man' (p. 155). Weber's modern world was thus characterized by a 'public world of separate, unattached, competing and contending individuals' which was served by a 'depoliticized private world of personal bonds and attachments – sustained by women's love and labour' (Bologh, 1990: 18). Holding out little hope for socialism as an emancipatory force, Weber foresaw little relief from relentless rationalization of the world, and saw the 'blush' of the Enlightenment fading away (Weber, 1905/1958: 182).

Weber's pessimism regarding societal rationalization was picked up in the work of the early Frankfurt School. Horkheimer and Adorno turned their attention to 'the specific logic of such spheres as the family, the state and culture in order to develop a more comprehensive analysis of the relation between the economic substructure, the superstructure, and the individual psyche' (Mills, 1987: 86–7). The central thrust of their work on the family was to demonstrate that 'the family not only depends on the historically concrete social reality, but is socially mediated down to its innermost structure' (Barrett and MacIntosh, 1982: 35). As Horkheimer and Adorno portrayed it, the increasing commodification of labour, spurred by capitalist accumulation processes, resulted in women being drawn into production and a weakening of traditional patriarchal family structures. Against Marx, who saw the entry of women into the productive realm and the decline of the bourgeois family as progressive, even as he railed against the transformation of women and children into economic instruments, Adorno and Horkheimer concentrated on the consequences of reduced ego autonomy and were forced to 'mourn the passing of the authoritarian father' (Whitebook, 1985: 147).[3] In their hands, the 'decline of subjectivity' resulting from the erosion of the private sphere became central: human beings had become so totally dominated that there was no possibility of emancipatory struggle.

To summarize, in the wake of the upheavals of modernity,

classical sociology tried to come to terms with the individual–society paradox. In opposition to utilitarian individualism, which sets up a clear opposition between individual and society, classical theory tries to resolve that opposition, reversing the ontological priority given to the individual in liberal theory (Yeatman, 1986). The sociological individual is born, created only through the social context. As Durkheim (1893/1933: 37) phrased his question 'Why does the individual, while becoming more autonomous, depend more on society? How can he be at once more individual and more solitary?'. Marx perceived a similar paradox in the *Grundrisse*: 'It is not until the eighteenth century, in bourgeois society, that the various forms of the social nexus confront the individual as merely a means towards his private ends, as external necessity. But the epoch which produces this standpoint, that of the isolated individual, is precisely the epoch of the hitherto most highly developed social relations' (Marx, 1857–8/1973: 83–4). For Weber, it is the modern individual caught inextricably in the 'iron cage'[4] who suggests the double-edged sword of individuation and domination. Modernity, then, gives sociology its subject – the individual who is at once autonomous and socially determined. Yet the classical project never realized the promise in this basic premise for the theorization of all aspects of social life. By consigning women to the 'natural', the 'pre-social', the 'primary group' or the 'embryo of community', gender itself was effectively written out of the purview of the 'socially created'.

1.2 Contemporary Theories of Modernity: Giddens and Habermas

The disappearance of women from the realm of the social is not a quirk of Victorian classical theorists, but is replicated in even the most recent contributions to the discourse of modernity. For example, the two contemporary theorists who best represent the continuation of the classical project of modernist social theory – Anthony Giddens and Jürgen Habermas – have constructed 'grand theories' of society and social change in which gender is barely mentioned.

Bryant and Jary (1991: 1) remark that 'sociology does not know quite what to make of Anthony Giddens and his theory of structuration'. He is, as they suggest, 'too big to be ignored, and too singular to be labelled with confidence'. The difficulty of summarizing Giddens's theory is complicated by the sheer volume of his output since the 1970s and by the supradisciplinary nature of his work. Poggi (1990) suggests that, in fact, there are really two Giddenses, the 'exegetical Giddens', and 'the structuration theorist' (p. 11). While I, like Poggi, find the exegetical Giddens more compelling, it is his elaboration of structuration theory that I shall focus on here. Drawing on an eclectic range of theoretical traditions (including, but not limited to, Marxism, phenomenology, linguistic philosophy and hermeneutics), Giddens's structuration theory incorporates both an extensive set of methodological rules and an analysis of various institutional articulations in modern society. If there is anything one can point to as the 'core' of his theory, it is what he calls the 'duality of structure'. By this, he means that structures are 'the medium and outcome of the practices they recursively organize. Structure is not "external" to individuals . . . .Structure is not to be equated with constraint, but is always both constraining and enabling' (Giddens, 1984: 25). It is with the duality of structure that Giddens seeks to replace the dualism of structure and agency that has plagued social theory. To examine the structuration of social practices, then, is to 'seek to explain how it comes about that structures are constituted through action, and reciprocally how action is constituted structurally' (Giddens, 1976: 161). Structuration occurs across time and space: institutions are social practices which 'stretch' across time and space, and this is how social systems are 'reproduced'. 'The structural practices of social systems "bind" the temporality of the *durée* of the day-to-day life world to the *longue durée* of institutions, interpolated in the finite span of existence of the individual human being' (Giddens, 1981: 28). It is Giddens's institutional analysis of modern society that grounds his sociology of modernity. The institutional dimensions of modernity include capitalism, industrialism, surveillance ('control of information and social supervision') and military power ('control of the means of violence in the context of the industrialization of war') (Giddens, 1990: 59). While these dimensions overlap, they are analytically distinct, and have independent consequences.

In five works on Giddens – three edited collections (Bryant and Jary, 1991; Clark, Modgil and Modgil, 1990; Held and Thompson, 1989) and two monographs (Ira Cohen, 1989; Craib, 1992) – only one essay takes up the exclusion of gender in Giddens's structuration theory in any serious fashion (Murgatroyd, 1989). Murgatroyd takes Giddens to task for his omission of 'half of society (and the relationship between that half and the other half)' (p. 147). As he builds a picture of social institutions and social relations on this faulty foundation, it is difficult, she suggests, 'to imagine where institutions such as families or households fit into his conception' (p. 152). The shortcomings of his institutional analysis are brought into sharp relief by his one-dimensional conception of what liberation for women might mean. This weakness runs through both his earlier and his later works. In *The Class Structure of the Advanced Societies* (1973), he excuses himself from having to deal seriously with stratification on the basis of gender: 'Given that women still have to await their liberation from the family it remains the case in capitalist societies that female workers are largely peripheral to the class system' (p. 288). He may thus neatly sidestep the relationship between 'the family' and 'the class structure'. In *Modernity and Self-Identity* (1991) he briefly discusses feminism as an example of 'life politics', casting 'liberation' as escape from family and domesticity and the negotiation of new self-identities in the public realm. This, too, rests on an inadequate theorization of the relationship between spheres.

In his contribution to the Held and Thompson reader (1989), Giddens generally accepts that he has not accorded sufficient attention to gender, but sees structuration theory as adequate to the task with little modification. He cites here, as elsewhere, Connell's work (1987) as the sort of gender-focused analysis that structuration theory might inform (e.g. Giddens, 1991: 215–16). While Connell has usefully drawn on structuration theory in developing a feminist-informed analysis, as has Felski (1989b), he has not done so uncritically. What emerges as most useful for feminists out of Giddens's work is the vocabulary of structuration, which allows for a dynamic theorization of the relationship between structure and agency. Giddens's substantive sociology of modernity is less useful. His attempts to come to grips with the 'shattering impact of modernity' (Giddens, 1989: 301) have paid only the most marginal attention to gender as constituting the social practices and structures that are implicated across time and space. Furthermore, as a number of critics suggest, Giddens's insistence on the openness of structuration processes leave questions of the political implications of structuration theory unanswered (or rather, unasked). Thompson (1989: 75) correctly notes that 'while social structure is reproduced and transformed by action, it is also the case that the range of options available to individuals and groups of individuals are differentially distributed and structurally circumscribed'. As Craib (1992: 185–6) summarizes the problem, Giddens' 'overassertion of human freedom leads to the failure to establish or found a moral critique'. For a theory of modernity which asserts the necessity of developing such a critique, we can look to Jürgen Habermas.

Habermas's 'break' with the earlier Frankfurt theorists was in part based on the abandonment of the Enlightenment that their position characterized. Rooting his critique of Marx and Weber, as well as of Horkheimer and Adorno, in their inability to separate clearly different categories of rationality, Habermas develops a model of social evolution in which different types of rationality operate at different levels and through different actions. The most crucial distinction is between purposive (instrumental) rationality, geared to exchange and control, and based on a subject–object relationship, and communicative rationality, geared towards understanding and based on a subject–subject relationship. Habermas grants that the 'utopia of reason' formed in the Enlightenment has never been fulfilled by modernity. It is not modernity *per se* which has suppressed reason, however, but its one-sided development as instrumental rationality which has blocked the potential of the communicative infrastructure, which has, in his words, 'buried alive' possibilities for expression' (Habermas, 1981/1987a: 329). Modernity is thus 'an unfinished project' and one which 'must create its normativity out of itself' (Habermas, 1987b: 7). Habermas finds cultural modernism to be the basis for an 'historically enlightened consciousness', the 'only resource we can still creatively draw on' (1986: 107).

Habermas has described his overall project as a 'reconstruction of historical materialism' (1976/1979: 95), which he takes to be 'a theory of society with a practical intent' (1971/1974: 3). He criticizes Marx for reducing all human praxis to labour, and reconstructs historical materialism to reflect a distinction between labour and interaction. This distinction is elaborated as a more complex evolutionary process, embracing both technical control over objective processes (labour) and communicative understanding through participation in symbolic interaction (interaction). His insistence on communicative rationality as a 'collective learning process' inserts a moral dimension into the theory. Thus he proposes that historical materialism must be reconstructed on a reconceptualized relationship between system integration, based on instrumental rationality, and social integration, based on communicative rationality, with the latter centred in the 'lifeworld'. The lifeworld is the locus of cultural reproduction, and thus represents the intersection of structure and agency. For Habermas, the separation of system and lifeworld is a historical process.

Habermas's evolutionary model is based on a progression of 'principles of organization'. In 'primitive' social formations, it is the kinship system, with its matrix of age and sex roles, which determines the 'totality of social intercourse' (Habermas, 1973/1975: 18). In 'traditional' social formations, class domination in its political form becomes the principle of organization. 'With the rise of a bureaucratic apparatus of authority, a control centre is differentiated out of the kinship system. . . .The kinship system is no longer the institutional nucleus of the whole system: it surrenders the central functions of power and control to the state' (1973/1975: 18–19). In this stage, social integration and system integration become differentiated. In the liberal–capitalist social formation, 'unpolitical' class rule, based on the relationship of wage-labour and capital, is the principle of organization. The political and the economic become 'uncoupled', enabling the economic system to contribute to both system and social integration. This is possible because 'in liberal capitalism the class relationship is institutionalized through the labour market and is thereby depoliticized' (1975: 25). There is a corresponding evolution of normative structures, following a developmental logic from the particular to the universal. As Lawrence (1989: 151–2) summarizes it:

Historically, normative structures which were based on substantive ethics – as in feudalism – could engender legal norms which gave

privileges and rights to certain strata but denied them to others.
However, such structures depend for their validity on world views
which presuppose either divine revelation or objective values
. . .[T]he mode of economic activity characteristic of capitalism
necessitated a universalist justification.

In late capitalism, the political and the economic become
'recoupled', as the state now goes beyond merely securing the
conditions of production (as in liberal capitalism), but is actively
engaged in it. Economic and state systems are not simply detached
from the lifeworld, but imbedded in it. There is no simple division
between 'public' and 'private'.

As Fraser (1989: 123) suggests, there are a number of advantages
to eliminating the dualistic separation of 'public' and 'private'. To
summarize, this approach treats the modern, restricted nuclear
family as historically emergent, with its own determinate factors; it
specifies that this type of family emerges in relation to the emerging
capitalist economy and administrative state, and it charts the
dynamics of exchange between them. This is a distinct improve-
ment on the classical constructions of the public–private division as
running *between* the family and the economy and polity. Yet
Habermas's model suffers from his lack of attention to kinship and
gender relations as organizing principles in the modern age, which
leads to questions arising about his relevance to feminist theory.
Most significantly, as Fraser points out, Habermas has failed to
theorize the 'gender subtext' by neglecting the gendered character
of modernity. Gender becomes invisible in the complexities of
material and symbolic reproduction, confined to particularity and
privacy. If the gender subtext is elaborated:

> [I]t then becomes clear that feminine and masculine gender identity
> run like pink and blue threads through the areas of paid work, state
> administration and citizenship as well as through the domain of
> familial and sexual relations. This is to say that gender identity is
> lived out in all arenas of life. It is. . .a basic element of the social
> glue that binds them to one another (Fraser, 1989: 127–8).

Where Habermas delineates the roles of worker and consumer as
linking the family to the economy and the roles of citizen and client
as linking it to the public sphere and the state, he fails to see that

these are inherently gendered roles. Thus, as Fraser asserts, the concepts of worker, consumer and wage are 'gender-economic' concepts, as is citizenship a 'gender-political' concept. By failing to see the gendered character of the social differentiation which underpins his theorization of modernity, Habermas blocks the analysis of some crucial issues. As Fraser (1989: 137) summarizes it: 'The struggles and wishes of contemporary women are not adequately clarified by a theory that draws the battle line between system and lifeworld institutions. From a feminist perspective, there is a more basic battle line between the forms of male dominance linking "system" and "lifeworld" *and us*.'

Cohen and Arato (1992: 543), in agreement with Fraser, contend that 'The largest gap in Habermas's work is his failure to consider the gendered character of the roles of worker and client that emerged along with the differentiation of the market economy and the modern state from the lifeworld.' I would argue that this gap is not merely Habermas's but the failing of theories of modernity more generally. Thus, in both classical and contemporary theoretical accounts of modernity, gender is located in the realm of kinship and family, a sphere of social life which has great import in the structuring of 'pre-modern' social formations, but loses this importance as an organizing principle as 'modern' society develops. Once industrialized, capitalized class society is introduced into history, women and children disappear. As modernity created the modern 'man', women were left behind. The construction of what is human is implicitly male, white, ruling class and Western, and largely based on a reification of economic individualism. Joan Landes (1984: 21) summarizes the ambivalent relationship of women to modernity well:

> On the one hand, woman, like nature, provided a moral antidote to the worst abuses of civilization. . . .[W]omen's virtue could offer a justification for her necessary privatization. How else could her spirituality, innocence or purity be preserved? On the other hand, woman as nature inhibited the progressive side of society and its rational reconstruction. Insofar as woman represented a backward, traditional, irrational force, she had to be controlled, contended with and contained.

From a feminist perspective, then, failure of theories of modernity more generally has been their inability to come to terms with sexual difference – to theorize particularity in a way which does not ignore, obscure or alienate the experience of women.

1.3   The End of Modernity? Feminism and Postmodernism

The feminist critique is frequently cited as good reason for the transcendence of the modern paradigm and for the emergence of a postmodern sociology. 'Postmodernism', of course, embraces a heterogeneous body of theory, grouping together theories not necessarily any more commensurable than Durkheim and Marx are in the 'modernist' grouping. The term 'postmodernism' itself has had a remarkable trajectory, from architecture through aesthetic and literary theory into social theory.[5] There are, however, certain shared attitudes which distinguish a postmodern position, and I shall use the term here to refer to the work of theorists such as Lyotard (1984), Baudrillard (1983) and Foucault (1980). The most basic of the shared attitudes towards postmodernism is, contra Habermas, that we should not aspire to complete the 'project of modernity' – that it is unfinished 'because its completion is inconceivable, and its value is increasingly open to question' (Smart, 1992: 183).

Modernity, the postmodern voice says, is about conquest. Modernity, it charges, is about silencing others in a sort of theoretical imperialism. The prefix 'post-' is deployed to signify a break with modernity and its Enlightenment heritage, so that the assertion inherent in the term postmodernism is that we have entered a qualitatively new era, one which requires a fundamental rethinking of social science. The postmodern landscape is character-ized by de-differentiation and by fading boundaries between image and reality. The very notion of the 'social' becomes problematic, calling into question the relevance of a discipline like sociology. The postmodern critique forswears the 'master discourses' of the Enlightenment in favour of local stories. It criticizes modernity's aspirations of universality, instead valorizing difference and heterogeneity. Postmodernism distrusts reason, unmasking it as a weapon used to exclude and to silence.

There would seem to be, as many have suggested, a natural affinity between postmodernism and feminism, given their shared suspicions about the Enlightenment legacy. Flax (1987: 624) characterizes feminist theory as a 'type of postmodern philosophy' which joins with other postmodern philosophies to raise 'important metatheoretical questions about the possible nature and status of theorizing itself'. Nicholson (1992: 93) suggests that 'Feminists can produce better theory. . .by more consistently abiding by their postmodern inclinations.' These 'inclinations' include the postmodern scepticism regarding any notion of a coherent subject, the rejection of science as objective truth and the disavowal of the universalizing impulses of modernity. The challenge of the postmodern attitude is a considerable one, and one which cannot be countered (or ignored) merely by appealing to the authority of 'reason' embodied in the master discourses of the Enlightenment legacy, for such reason rests on an assumption of a universal subject which both feminist and postmodernist critiques have unmasked as a fiction. Yet an uncritical adoption of a postmodern stance raises some crucial questions for feminism. Is 'postmodernity' any more relevant as a periodizing framework than 'modernity' for women? Where, exactly, is the break between modern and postmodern? What difference has this break wrought for the way in which the majority of the world's women live their lives? As Kellner (1990: 268–9) suggests, postmodern theories tend to exaggerate 'the novelty of the contemporary moment and occlude continuities with the past' in a manner reminiscent of earlier post-industrial theories:

Both postmodern theories and those of the post-industrial society. . .make technological development the motor of social change and occlude the extent to which economic imperatives, or a dialectic between technology and the mode of production, continue to structure contemporary societies. Both erase human subjects and social classes as agents of social change and both explicitly renounce hope for radical social change. . . .They take trends as constitutive facts, and developmental possibilities as finalities, and both assume that a possible future is already present.

Others, such as Nancy Hartsock (1987: 196), are sceptical about the timing of the 'postmodern revolution' in theory:

Why is it, exactly at the moment when so many of us who have been silenced begin to demand the right to name ourselves, to act as subjects rather than objects of history, that just then the concept of subjecthood becomes problematic? Just when we are forming our own theories about the world, uncertainty emerges about whether the world can be adequately theorized? Just when we are talking about the changes we want, ideas of progress and the possibility of 'meaningfully' organizing human society become suspect?

How can theory which decries the systematic be useful for those who need to understand the world systematically? Are we abandoning tools for understanding increasingly global interdependencies just when we need them most? (Antonio, 1990: 108). Postmodern theories tend to fall back on some notion of reason, humanness, reality — that is, they deny that there is any reality while simultaneously telling us how things really are. In this sense, do they not replicate the gender-saturated categories of the Enlightenment heritage that they denounce? While we might value the contribution that postmodern theories have made towards problematizing many basic theoretical assumptions, feminists must nevertheless proceed with caution or risk finding themselves marginalized by yet another important theoretical turn.

As Marshall Berman (1988: 24) notes, while classical theorists looked at gains and losses and the ambiguities of modernity, contemporary theory has tended to treat modernity as a 'closed monolith', either uncritically embraced or unilaterally condemned. The postmodern critique rightly problematizes assumptions of social theory — it opens opportunities to rewrite the script, but does not do so in a useful way. Thus I want to suggest that we do need to problematize modernity, but we do not need to abandon its project altogether. I think it is mistaken to call any position which is critical of modernity or of Enlightenment thought 'post-modern'. To do so ignores the self-critical moment of modernity. Habermas, the foremost defender of the 'project of modernity', refers to the '*counter*-discourse which has inhabited modernity ever since the beginning' and suggests that 'there is no cure for the wounds of the Enlightenment other than the radicalized Enlightenment itself' (1986: 158). Rather than abandoning the notion of 'modernity' altogether, there is much to be gained in building on the critical impulse which has always inhabited it. But it is not enough to criticize the incompletion of the project of modernity – we must scrutinize the principles on which the project itself is based. This scrutiny must begin with some reflection on the implications of the basic analytical framework which has shaped the sociological theorization of modernity.

1.4 Conclusions: Capitalism, Modernity and the Theorization of Gender

As Sayer (1991: 1) notes, it is the analysis of capitalism – the central preoccupation of social theory since the eighteenth century social theory – which has grounded the most influential sociological theories of modernity.[6] Modern capitalist society produced a uniquely modern individual, one created by and bound up in new forms of social relationships. For classical theory, this unique form of 'sociation' (Sayer, 1991: 2) is that nexus of relationships which derive from the changes wrought by industrial capitalism – most significantly, the increasingly specialized division of labour, the expansion of science and technical rationality to encompass more and more aspects of life, the economic dominance of wage labour and commodity production and the emergence of a political citizenry. While this focus has been a fruitful one, it has also limited the field of vision. The theoretical canon has directed our gaze to the visibly public realms of economics and politics, where 'modern man' emerged. It has also nourished, particularly in the tradition of Marxist theory, a skewed vision of what a better human future might look like – a vision informed in Marxism by what Benhabib and Cornell (1987: 3) call 'emancipation through the liberation of work'. The grand narrative of historical materialism rests on labour as its basic ontological category. This fundamental tenet is challenged by feminism and by other social struggles which cannot be reduced to the labour–capital relationship. The gendered division of labour is the most visible manifestation of a far deeper opposition of 'female' and abstract individualism, and it is at the same time cause and consequence of this opposition.

The classical focus on the relationship between capitalism and individualism has also provided an opening for a conservative assertion that 'capitalism promotes the economic and political

freedom of persons, and so defends the individual against the state'
(Abercrombie, Hill and Turner, 1986: 3). Debates about this
connection reverberate with a 'return to a nostalgic past where
gender difference. . .lies at the heart of social organization'
(Rothenberg, 1990: 54). This same past, although perhaps treated
with less longing in theoretical circles than in political discourse, is
part of the story of modernity in the classical project. The
sociological theorization of gender has relied heavily on the
'modernization' story – the differentiation of spheres, the increasing
division of labour, the separation of public and private spheres, the
'functional' specialization of women in 'reproductive' work. This
has been at the expense of a more adequate consideration of the
potential of modernity to imagine new possibilities for women,
which would entail working through the double-edged character of
the differentiation of spheres, seeing openings for new means and
contexts of identity formation.

There is warrant here for seeing similarities in the *fin-de-siècle*
angst both of nineteenth- and twentieth-century theoretical
projects. As Waerness (1984: 67) notes, the quality of social
relationships, loneliness and lack of fellowship are considered
something new; current public debate neglects the degree to which
these issues have constituted the central concerns of social theory for
centuries. It is thus the interpretation of modernity and its
dilemmas that comprises the battleground for debate, both
theoretical and political. Calls for the defence of the 'private sphere'
from both sides of the political spectrum, including some feminists,
have entered the literature (Berger and Berger, 1983; Donzelot,
1980; Elshtain, 1981; Lasch, 1979). Benjamin (1988: 201) calls
them 'gender conservatives', who take up 'defending the traditional
female ethos of nurturance while affirming its exclusion from the
public social world'. The blurring of boundaries between traditionally feminine and masculine personalities and orientations is
associated with the demise of the private sphere. Thus, feminist
proposals to 'de-gender' the childrearing role, restructuring its
relationship to other social activities, are 'transformed into a
nightmare vision of raising children like Perdue chickens' (Benjamin, 1988: 204).

It has always been real social changes that have presented the
issues with which theorists must grapple; previous accounts of social

life must have their lacunae and contradictions exposed. Women's struggle for autonomy, continually thwarted by the opposition of femininity and individuality, demands a fundamental reconsideration of the relationship between individual and society. Such a reconsideration must begin with some of the most basic categories that we have used to understand this relationship.

In the next chapter, I will argue that many contemporary accounts (socialist, feminist or otherwise) of the division of labour, and of the struggle between different economic and political interests that have shaped the current political and theoretical agenda, have crucially misunderstood the role of gender in organizing social life. In both classical and contemporary debates, the important axis of discussion has been the relationship between 'public' and 'private' spheres of social life, largely framed in terms of the opposition between them. I want to draw out the 'gender subtext' of these debates. It is through this process that we can understand the relationship between public and private spheres as something distinct from the gendered division of labour, and relate it back to the classical questions of the individual–society relationship.

2
Rethinking the Gendered Division
of Labour

The division of labour is a central issue in the theorization of modernity. More than anything else, it was the increasingly specialized, rationalized division of labour which accompanied industrial capitalism that framed some of the key questions for classical sociological theory. It was, however, the changing face of labour in the public realm of the official economy – men's labour – that was seen as 'modern', and as grounding a new relationship between the individual and society. The naturalization of women and their labour in the private realm established a fundamentally different relationship between women and modernity, setting up a deep-rooted association between a public–private split and a sexual division of labour. Both the theoretical and the political implications of this sort of understanding of the division of labour are profound. It makes the consideration of all aspects of social life, and hence a truly inclusive theorization of the individual–society relationship, impossible.

The division of labour continues to provide a compelling conceptual framework for organizing gender divisions, simply because the allocation and structuring of activities on the basis of sex is a universal phenomenon. As Hartsock (1985: 232) notes: 'Women's work in every society differs systematically from men's. . . .This division of labour is the first, and in some societies the only, division of labour; moreover it is central to the

organization of the social division of labour more generally.
all societies differentiate between 'men's work' and 'women's
there is considerable variation, both historically and cultu
with respect to what tasks are considered appropriate for each sex,
and in the degree of rigidity of the sex-typing of various activities.
For many theorists, the sexual division of labour is almost
synonymous with women's subordination, 'because it appears to
express, embody, and furthermore to perpetuate, female subordination' (Mackintosh, 1981: 2).

Certainly, understanding the sexual division of labour is crucial
to understanding women's oppression, but what is important is *how*
we understand this division. In this chapter, I want to discuss a
number of issues related to this problem. First, I will review
evidence of divisions of labour between men and women — between
waged and unwaged labour, within waged labour, and within
unwaged labour. Secondly, I will review some of the theoretical
work which has sought to explain the persistence of these divisions,
and which has underscored the fact that it is a gendered division of
labour with which we must be concerned, and not, strictly
speaking, a sexual one. Finally, I will attempt to relate the
theoretical significance of some of the trends in the gendered
division of labour to the overall problematic of the reproduction of
gender inequality. Linking the analysis to the gender–work–class
debates, I want to demonstrate that the conflation of the division of
labour between men and women with a division of social life into
public and private spheres is both theoretically and politically
untenable. Thus, while Mann (1986: 56) contends that 'stratification is now gendered', I will argue that it always has been. I will
argue for a reconceptualized relationship between gender, labour,
kinship and modernity — one which recognizes the fundamental
changes wrought in both public and private spheres, and the
relationship between them.

2.1 The Gendered Division of Labour

Early anthropological work established the division of labour
between the sexes as a universal yet variable phenomenon. Since
then, many researchers have documented the extent and form of the

gendered division of labour in both national and international contexts. Research has focused primarily on the division between 'men's jobs' and 'women's jobs' in the paid labour market, and on the broader division between paid and unpaid labour, with an emphasis on women's unwaged labour in the home. Less frequently discussed, but also salient, are gendered divisions within unwaged labour.

2.1.1   *Divisions between waged and unwaged labour*

Marsden (1981), taking a poke at the traditional categories of labour market analysis, suggests that those who work *only* for wages should be considered 'secondary workers'. In doing so, she neatly drives home the fact that women, as a group, perform substantially more work than men as a group, yet receive far less in the way of financial compensation. The main reason for this, of course, is that most of women's work is unwaged.

In most industrialized nations, women have become increasingly involved in waged labour during the twentieth century, significantly closing the gap between their participation in the paid labour force and men's (Bakker, 1988; OECD, 1985; A. Scott, 1986). Women have accounted for most of the growth in the labour force, with participation by men showing a decline. There is clearly a life-cycle pattern to the movement of women between unwaged labour and participation in both unwaged and waged labour. Marsden (1981: 58–9) sums up the career of the 'main worker':

> The typical main worker enters main work after the completion of his/her education and, throughout life until death, combines main and secondary work, sometimes exclusively in one or the other but always, potentially, in both. The worker typically begins as a secondary worker only. . . .[A]t marriage or co-habitation, this person becomes a main worker contributing both in secondary labour for about 40 hours a week and in the domestic and community sphere about 30 or more hours a week. . . .Perhaps the most important contribution of the main worker's life is the preparation of the next generation of workers. This used to be considered main work on its own, but increasingly. . .main workers are also picking up the load of secondary labour. The typical main

worker, however. . .has a clear set of priorities when it comes to contribution to the society and concentrates for several years when children are young on their proper socialization to our society.

While women comprise a minority of paid workers, there is no doubt that they constitute the vast majority of unpaid workers. Research on domestic labour in several countries (Berk, 1985; Hochschild, 1989; Luxton, 1990; Pahl, 1984) shows that women, whether or not they also have paid jobs, remain responsible for most of the work associated with household maintenance and child-rearing. Women also do unwaged work as 'unpaid family workers', particularly in agriculture and small business (Pamela Smith, 1987; Westwood and Bhachu, 1988). Another form of unwaged labour performed almost exclusively by women is that involved in main-taining what has been termed the 'two-person' career (Papanek, 1973). Whether she is typing papers for an academic, entertaining a businessman's colleagues or posing for photographs with a politician, the wife who is 'incorporated' into her husband's career (Finch, 1983) performs labour which is unwaged and unrecognized, even by the category of 'unpaid family worker'. It is difficult to estimate the number of hours involved in such labour, as it varies widely and has received relatively little attention in the literature.[1] Finally, no accounting of unwaged work would be complete without mentioning the vast amount of volunteer work done in the community by women (Ross, 1990; Vellekoop-Baldock, 1990).

To summarize, then, there is an unequal distribution of total labour time between men and women, with women as a group performing more labour overall than men as a group. Men perform a greater proportion of waged labour, while women perform a greater proportion of unwaged labour as domestic workers, as unpaid family workers, as labourers contributing directly to their husband's paid work and as volunteers.

2.1.2   Divisions within waged labour

Whether we look at occupations, industries, hours of work or wage levels, persistent divisions between men and women are found in the paid labour market in most industrialized nations (Bakker, 1988; Crompton and Sanderson, 1990; A. Scott, 1986). By occupation, women tend to be located within a narrow range of jobs, most notably in clerical, sales and service work. Looking at hours of work, we find a far greater proportion of women than men in part-time employment.

As labour history shows us, significant changes in the gender composition of the labour force tend to come about primarily with changes in technology (Cockburn, 1985; Lowe, 1987) and/or requirements for new sources of labour as the economy develops and restructures – good examples here are clerical work (Davies, 1982; Lowe, 1987), nursing (Garmanikov, 1978) and teaching (Prentice, 1977). In the current wave of industrial restructuring, we find new developments in the division and redivision of labour which are inherently gendered. Two examples of this sort of gendered 'redivision' that merit mention here are the use of women as a cheap, flexible labour force by 'runaway capital' in the rapidly industrializing Third World, and in the move towards more industrial outworking and part-time or casual work in advanced capitalist economies.

The term 'the new international division of labour' has gained currency in describing the relocation of jobs from the highly industrialized West to newly industrialized, low-wage countries in Asia and Latin America. It is a reversal of the traditional pattern of labour moving to capital. Mitter (1986: 9) estimates that between 1971 and 1983 one and a half million workers, mostly women, lost their jobs in the clothing and textiles industry in Europe and the USA, while more than two million women workers found jobs in the clothing and textile industries in the Third World. In the growing microelectronics industries, the labour-intensive operations, such as assembly, are being shifted to low-wage countries where women are recruited as the new workers. Pearson (1988) demonstrates the variability, yet underlying similarity, in the use of female labour in low-wage countries as capital seeks to maximize profits through the use of cheap female labour while staying in harmony with the traditional patriarchal ideologies of the culture. Some employers look for women who are childless and may require pregnancy tests as a condition of employment, some prefer women who have had their children and are past childbearing age, some pay the women's wages to her father or husband, others allow traditional leaders onto the production line to check the modesty of the company uniform. As Pearson concludes, 'there are a range of production relations which vary according to the historically determined situation of women in any given situation' (p. 455).

While global economic restructuring is creating new feminized labour markets in the Third World, redivision continues in the advanced industrial states. 'Rationalization' of production processes, the growth of the service sector and privatization of government services are indicative of this gendered redivision of labour. As industry seeks to lower its labour costs, full-time, continuing employment is increasingly supplanted by part-time and/or limited contract employment. Industrial outworking continues to be performed by an overwhelmingly female, often immigrant female, labour force. For example, the British National Homeworking Study in 1981 estimated homeworkers at approximately 8 per cent of the labour force, with women making up 71 per cent of all homeworkers (Hakim, 1988: 611–4). In her discussion of the impact of new technologies on women's work, Armstrong (1984: 167) suggests that 'There is clearly enormous potential for increasing the number of paid jobs done at home and most of those who will see their work transformed in this way are women.' In support of this assertion, she cites 'a representative from a major employer of female clerical workers', speaking at a conference in 1982, as claiming 'that his company was now in a position to make half of its clerical jobs homework jobs'.

Privatization of government services also means a shift from full-time, high-wage jobs to part-time, low-wage and often contractually limited employment done overwhelmingly by women. Post office privatization in Canada, for example, has replaced some of the few high-paying jobs for women in rural areas with minimum-wage jobs in private enterprises, for instance as shop assistants. Similar trends are apparent in health services, child-care and social services.

In summary, the historically entrenched division of labour between men and women in the paid labour force is continually created, through new divisions and redivisions as the economy restructures. It cannot be viewed as a division merely 'inherited' by capitalism. As Connell (1987: 102) puts it: 'We are dealing not just with the allocation of work, but with the nature and organization of that work.' Gender divisions are built into the paid labour market, and continue to shape its development.

2.1.3   *Divisions within unwaged labour*

It is only recently that scholars have taken significant interest in unwaged labour, and it has been suggested that the burgeoning interest in the 'informal' sphere and the 'household economy' is related to the increased importance of male's unwaged labour. As Delphy and Leonard (1986: 235) put it: 'Only with the recent profound changes in capitalism and the massive rise in male unemployment, with the associated growth in men's involvement in non-market activities, has there been concern with this sector of the economy and a recognition of the vast nature of its scale.' Studies of the 'informal economy' and 'household strategies' have focused on the household as a unit which seeks to maximize its resources through a mix of waged and unwaged labour. As the assurance of the availability of waged labour is increasingly threatened by changing economic conditions, the importance of unwaged labour to household survival increases.

We have already noted that women perform the bulk of unwaged labour. Yet, within unwaged labour, there remain distinct divisions between men's work and women's work. Most notably, gendered divisions are entrenched in household work and 'caring' labour.

Household work has not been unaffected by industrial and economic changes. Ruth Schwartz Cowan titled her historical survey of the impact of technology on household work *More work for mother* (1983). The first domestic tasks to be eliminated by their commercialization or innovations in technology were tasks traditionally allocated to men — such as chopping and hauling wood, home shoe-making, mending ironware and butchering. 'For women, the transition to the industrial order was different. Merchant flour, cast-iron stoves, municipal water, and manufactured boots did not free them from their labours. Insofar as these commodities allowed men and boys to leave their homes, and insofar as these commodities also created new jobs that only women could perform, women were tied even more strongly than they had been before to their cast-iron hearths' (Cowan, 1983: 67).

Men's participation in domestic work continues to be substantially different from that of women's, and not only in the sense that they spend far less time doing it. In summarizing the research on the division of labour within the household, Berk (1985: 9) notes that men have a distinct preference in their household work for tasks which are 'functionally specific' (i.e. they have 'identifiable components and well-defined boundaries', such as mowing the lawn), tasks which allow discretion in when and how they are performed (such as minor household repairs) or tasks which can be construed as 'active leisure' (such as gardening or playing with the children). The study by Luxton (1990) shows that men tend to take on specific, clearly bounded tasks and rarely participate in pre-task planning: 'For example, a number of men did the grocery shopping on a regular basis but they insisted that the woman draw up the basic list of things needed. Some men would do the laundry, if all the dirty clothes were previously collected and sorted and if the necessary soap and bleach were at hand' (p. 48). She also notes that men prefer jobs involving machinery, whether vacuuming or preparing meals with such tools as a food processor or microwave oven. The research by Cockburn (1985: 218) indicates that 'technology is just as significant a factor in the division of labour at home as it is at work', and she suggests that there is much gender-based ideological construction of what technology is considered appropriate to women (e.g. sewing machines) and what is appropriate to men (e.g. power drill). Thus, domestic labour becomes gender-divided in terms of the specificity, discretion and perceived level of technological skill attached to the task.

Unwaged 'caring' labour remains almost entirely the domain of women.[2] Graham (1983: 13) defines caring as 'that range of human experiences which have to do with feeling concern for, and taking charge of, the well-being of others'. While much domestic labour, such as cooking and doing laundry, can be construed as 'taking charge of the well-being of others', the notion of 'caring labour' implies more than the performance of certain tasks that enhance the well-being of others. 'Caring' is inextricably intertwined with traditional conceptions of femininity and with the moral interpretations of what constitutes a 'good woman' (Matthews, 1984; Ungerson, 1983). As unwaged labour, caring manifests itself most noticeably as the responsibility of women for the well-being of other members of their family, and in particular, dependent members, such as children and ill or elderly parents. That most states recognize the need for maternity leave, but not paternity or parental leave, bears witness to the deeply held assumption that care of infants and small children is best entrusted to those who physically bear them. That most states do not recognize the need for leave from paid employment to care for other types of dependants bears witness to the difficulty that exists in acknowledging caring *as* labour. The ideology of familialism defines caring as love, not labour. As Dalley (1988) notes, men are expected to care *about* (but not necessarily care *for*) their families by providing the physical setting and financial resources for caring labour to take place — labour usually performed by his wife. Men may participate in that labour through the performance of certain tasks, but as with domestic labour in general, the responsibility belongs to women. As a remarkable example of this type of gendered division in caring labour, Luxton (1990: 49) notes that men referred to 'baby-sitting' their own children, a term that women never used in that context.

2.1.4   Summary

It is clear that gender divisions are integral to the social division of labour in general. Whether we look at the division between waged and unwaged labour, or within waged or unwaged labour, gender persists as the main 'organizer' of work. Gendered divisions of labour do not seem to respect any neat division between 'public' and 'private', but run through all spheres. Nor are they 'feudal relics' (Corrigan, 1990: 54). They are actively and continuously created and re-created, both in 'public' and 'private'. This recognition has great significance for theorizing the gendered division of labour. As I will demonstrate in the rest of this chapter, prevailing theories of the division of labour, and of the gender, work and class relationship are fundamentally flawed by some of their basic assumptions. I will argue that they have tended: (a) to rest on a relatively narrow conception of 'labour'; (b) to neglect the degree to which gender divisions shape both the material and ideological forms that the division of labour takes; (c) to 'read back into history' (D. Smith, 1985) the separation of gender and economic processes, and thus reify both the public–private dualism and its coincidence with a gendered division of labour.

2.2 Theoretical Perspectives

While descriptive accounts of the division of labour between men and women abound, adequate explanations for these divisions are harder to come by. For the most part, sociological and economic studies of work have laboured under traditional assumptions about 'sex-roles' and, in particular, about 'work' and 'family' as opposing spheres, with women placed squarely in the latter. In doing so, these studies tend to mistake the consequences of the situation for its causes. Clearly indictable on this account are the functionalist sociological account of Parsons and Bales (1955) and the neoclassical economic approach. Yet these politically conservative approaches are not alone in their failings — much Marxist-influenced scholarship has replicated these assumptions in analysing the division of labour solely from the point of view of the 'needs of capital'. As Yanigasako and Collier (1987: 25) suggest, a 'means/end relationship' has dominated western sociological thought on the relationship between the family and capitalism, 'a means/end relationship between what they [sociologists] construe as the reproductive and productive spheres of capitalist-industrial society'. Explanations of the gendered division of labour can be grouped into three broad categories. First, there are approaches which focus on forces external to the labour market, such as structural functionalism in sociology and human capital theory in economics. Second are approaches which focus on forces within the capitalist labour market. Here I will look at segmented labour market theory and labour process theories. Finally, I will consider theories, in particular feminist theories, that emphasize an interplay of forces both external to and internal to the labour market.[3]

2.2.1 Extra-market forces

Of the approaches which target forces operating outside the wage labour market as primary in producing the gendered division of labour, the sociological account of Talcott Parsons and the human capital theory of neo-classical economists figure prominently.

The Parsonian view of role differentiation in the family must be placed in the context of Parsons's attempt to explain a variety of macro- and micro-level processes within a unified theoretical framework. Parsons was largely concerned with structural differentiation in industrial societies, and the individual–society link via processes of socialization and status attainment. The family becomes central to this analysis as an institution which performs certain functions which contribute to social stability. Parsons saw the domestic division of labour in the 1950s as a 'natural' consequence of 'role differentiation', which created a necessary interdependence among family members, contributing to the stability of the family as a social unit. Drawing heavily on Bales's small group research, he posited two distinct roles as necessary for small group functioning – the instrumental and expressive. The instrumental role is externally orientated towards goal-attainment and adaptation to the environment, while the expressive role is internally orientated towards integration and tension-management. It is via this role differentiation that the family is successfully articulated with the larger society while maintaining its own equilibrium. While it would be theoretically possible for both male and female to perform either role, Parsons suggested that women's biological role in childbearing naturally predisposes them to the expressive role. 'In our opinion the fundamental explanation of the allocation of the roles between the biological sexes lies in the fact that the bearing and early rearing of children established a strong presumptive primacy of the relation of mother to the small child and this in turn establishes a presumption that the man who is exempted from these biological functions, should specialize in the alternative instrumental direction' (Parsons and Bales, 1955: 23).

Parsons was primarily concerned with the American nuclear family of the 1950s. The adult male was expected to be the only member of the family with an occupational role; by providing economically for the other family members, he determined the social status of the family as a whole and linked the family unit to the larger society. The adult female's 'expressive' role was concerned with domestic maintenance, care of children and emotional support. Parsons was not unaware that women engaged in wage labour, but did not see this as invalidating his analysis, as the type of job a woman is likely to have 'tends to be of a qualitatively different type and not a status which seriously competes with that of her husband as the primary status-giver or income earner' (Parsons and Bales, 1955: 14).

What is significant in the Parsonian analysis is the splitting off of women from economic processes. He not only ignored the economic implications of women's wage labour, but of their domestic labour as well. Women's role in the family becomes one of cultural, not economic import (Beechey, 1987: 21). Once this 'theoretical sleight of hand' is accomplished, it is not difficult, as Middleton (1974: 180) suggests, to deny that women constitute a subordinate group at all. On the contrary, they fulfil a necessary and complementary role in a complex, structurally differentiated cultural system — 'different but equal'.

As married women's participation in wage labour greatly increased in the post-war period in most Western nations, the emphasis in mainstream sociology began to focus on the 'role strain' of married women in the work force. The employed woman, and in particular the employed mother, became ideologically constructed as a social problem. Feldberg and Glenn (1984) neatly capture this in their critique of the treatment of women in the sociology of work. They identify a tendency for studies of male workers to be conducted within a 'job model' — basic social relationships, social position, and socio-political attitudes are determined by work. For women, a 'gender model' is used, assuming their family position to be the primary determinant. The latter approach, in studies of women in paid employment, tends to 'emphasize the strains for women and their families resulting from women's "two jobs", while giving little consideration to the impacts of conditions of women's employment in specific jobs' (Feldberg and Glenn, 1984: 33). In addition, Beechey (1987) critiques studies of 'women's two roles' on the grounds that they share the functionalist preoccupation with normative expectations. The problem becomes 'reduced to individual role conflicts, with no explanation provided of their social foundations' (Beechey, 1987: 31).

'Human capital theory', while more popular in economics than sociology, has maintained a strong ideological foothold in explaining women's subordinate position in the labour market. Firmly rooted in functionalist assumptions about sex-role differentiation, it suggests that women accumulate less human capital — qualities such as training, experience, career commitment and allied qualities which are rewarded in the market – because they prefer to invest their time and energy in the expressive role within the family. Because their primary interest is their current, or expected, family role, they are less concerned with building up human capital; they 'choose' jobs which require less training, mobility and commitment, and which provide not only less opportunity for advancement but lower wages. Such a theory sits well with the ideology of a meritocracy, and is reflected in suggestions that women need only to build up their human capital to compete on an equal basis with men in the labour market. It sits less well with a more adequate analysis of the operation of the labour market, which suggests that women receive less return for their investment in human capital than men do, that the wage gap is largest in occupations with the lowest human capital requirements, and that men and women are constructed as crucially different labour forces.

2.2.2   Forces within the labour market

The failures of human capital theory have led to some version of segmented labour market theory as the new orthodoxy for explaining gender segregation in the labour market. The basis of segmented labour market theory is that the existence of divisions among the working class and within particular work-forces contributes to the development of capitalism as it facilitates employer control over their work-force. For example, Edwards (1979), in examining the changing structure of the US labour force, argues that three distinct labour markets have emerged: the primary, the subordinate primary and the secondary. These labour market segments are characterized by different labour processes, with varying levels of skill, wages and job security and different types of control. According to Edwards, race and sex differences among workers are used by employers to divide the working class, as women are increasingly directed into secondary labour markets with low security and rewards. This suggests that it was easier for capital to introduce altogether new labour power than to downgrade primary labour market workers; employment opportunities for women in the secondary labour market therefore expanded. While segmented labour market theory increases our understanding, from the system point of view, of the persistence of non-competing male and female labour forces, it is not without its problems. Faulty specification of labour market segments, for example, may mask important male–female differences within segments. Dex (1985) points out that in Edwards's schema, secretaries, nurses and craft workers are in the same labour market segment as managers and doctors! More importantly, the issue of gender inequality is described rather than adequately explained. A number of writers treating the clustering of women's occupations within certain labour market segments have concluded that the segmentation of occupations on the basis of gender was a result of both economic requirements of capital accumulation and patriarchal ideologies. In particular, Milkman (1983: 194) notes that gender divisions in industry persisted 'even in the face of a direct conflict with economic rationality'.

Similar problems plague work on the labour process. Labour process studies have taken the work-place as 'contested terrain' (Edwards, 1979) – the site of struggles between capital and labour, where each seeks to maximize their gain. Yet labour is construed as a gender-neutral category; as a result, work-place struggles are understood 'as bounded by the physical division between the factory and the outside world' (Greico and Whipp, 1986: 117). Feminist writers reviewing theories of the labour process have suggested that such a clear boundary cannot be drawn and that 'labour' is inherently a gendered category. Gender not only divides the work-force in a structural sense but impinges upon conceptualizations of skill (Phillips and Taylor, 1986), the use of technology (Cockburn, 1985; Hacker, 1989) and forms of authority and control (Kanter, 1977; Lown, 1983) in the work-place. Thomas (1982: 87) suggests that gender differences are 'more than merely ideological distinctions used to fragment politically an otherwise homogenous working class'; thus we must look at forces external to the labour process as integral in shaping the segmented labour market and the labour process.

2.2.3 *Interplay of market and non-market forces*

Two theoretical 'schools' can be located in this camp: the socio-economic approach of the Cambridge Labour Studies Group (Craig et al., 1985; Garnsey et al., 1985; Humphries and Rubery, 1984; Rubery, 1988), which examines the relationship between 'production' and 'social reproduction'; and more explicitly feminist approaches which analyse the relationship between capitalist and patriarchal forces (Delphy, 1984; Hartmann, 1979; Walby, 1986).

The approach of the Cambridge Group is an advance on earlier labour market segmentation theory in that it differentiates between the segmentation of the labour market (demand factors) and that of the labour force (supply factors). There is a recognition that men and women *supply* their labour on different terms. Thus 'the labour market position of women is not intrinsically vulnerable but is the result of the role specialization in the family and expectations which follow therefrom' (Garnsey et al., 1985: 59). Because this 'role specialization' in the family assigns the primary responsibility for family care and household maintenance to women, with the expectation that they will be party to income-sharing with a male wage-earner, 'many employers assume that women in general have lower income needs and lesser attachment to their jobs than men, even where in individual cases this assumption is inapplicable' (p. 60). It has been pointed out that 'men also have specific positions in the family which influence the terms on which they make their labour available on the market: for example, they may need to provide for dependants, and they may be free to work long and flexible hours because they can rely on others to provide the domestic labour they and their dependants require' (Craig et al., 1984: 95).

Supply and demand factors, then, condition each other. However, the basis for the extensiveness of 'role specialization' within the family, which is crucial in segmenting labour supply, remains largely unanalysed in this model. Feminist 'dual-systems' theories have tackled this question by examining patriarchy as the basis for this division of labour within the family.

The hallmark of feminist 'dual systems' theorizing is Hartmann's (1981: 18) assertion that 'capitalist development creates the places for a hierarchy of workers, but traditional Marxist categories cannot tell us who will fill which places. Gender and racial hierarchies determine who fills the empty places.' The concept of patriarchy is deployed to explain the origins of the gender hierarchy which fills the lowest spots in the capitalist hierarchy with women. Patriarchy, argues Hartmann, is based in men's control over women's labour, both paid and unpaid. Men's exclusionary practices in the labour market segregate women into low-wage jobs, enforcing their dependence on a male wage and thus their continued responsibility for domestic labour, and keeps them subordinate in the family. At the same time, men's control over women's labour in the domestic sphere reinforces their secondary status in the labour market, ensuring that the vicious circle continues. This relationship between capitalism and patriarchy benefits both men and capital. One takes care of demand, the other supply. According to Hartmann (1981), among others, patriarchy and capitalism find their common interest served by the 'family wage', which facilitates both occupational segregation and the assignment of domestic labour to women. A 'great conspiracy' between capitalists and men is suggested.

2.2.4 Summary

It is clear that gender has been a key factor in the development of the social division of labour, whether that labour is waged or unwaged. It is also clear that the most common explanation for this has been the identification of a link between the sexual division of labour in biological reproduction, the physical separation of home and work through industrialization, and the resulting gendered social division of labour. At the risk of an oversimplification, the basic argument can be summarized as follows: the fact that women physically bear children and have the capacity to breastfeed 'naturally' singles them out for child-rearing. This renders them less able to sell their labour in the 'public' sphere, and thus they must labour in 'private', for a male labourer who will share his wage with her. This basic relationship holds for whatever the theoretical formulation which is built on it. For Parsons, it results in a complementarity of 'expressive' and 'instrumental' roles in the family. For neoclassical economists, it accords women lower levels of human capital when they do enter the waged labour force, as their primary attachment is to the home. For Marxists, it serves the needs of the capitalist system by ensuring not only the efficient 'private' reproduction of workers, but a reserve army of labour. For feminists, it lays the basis for women's dependency on men as their primary source of livelihood – not for reasons of nature, but for the resulting patriarchal control of women's sexuality, and reproductive and productive labour. Central to most theoretical formulations is the association of women's labour with the private sphere and men's labour with the public sphere, and this division is, for most accounts, what is being reproduced. Thus, women's labour is undervalued because it occurs in the realm of reproduction (i.e. both biological and of the labour force), which is considered to be outside the relations of production proper, or merely to mimic reproductive work in the labour force. Yet it is the ever familiar formulation of men engaged in production and women in reproduction that I wish to question here. Instead, I will suggest that the 'public man'–'private woman' dualism is an abstraction which cannot be sustained, and that in fact what is being reproduced is the *conflation* of the sexual division of labour with the public–private division through this abstraction. Nowhere is this conflation more apparent than in the recent debates around the place of gender within class analysis.

2.3   Gender, Work and Class

Class analysis has remained the backbone of stratification theory and research; processes of class formation, empirical specification of class locations, and the potential for class action to transform, rather than reproduce, the underlying structure of class inequality have all been widely debated. Increasingly, the inability of class analysis to deal adequately with gender as a fundamental dimension of inequality in capitalist societies has called into question the adequacy of class-based models of social reproduction. Conventional class analysis has assumed that women derive their class position from that of the male head of the household (as indicated by their occupation). Consequently, the rather confusing label of 'women and class analysis' has been given to discussions of the position of women within the family, and in particular, the empirical difficulties of selecting the appropriate unit for class analysis, given that many women work both inside and outside the home (see for example, Goldthorpe, 1983, 1984; Heath and Britten, 1984; Stanworth,

1984). The debate about unit of analysis is not primarily methodological, despite the fact that it is often couched in such terms. More accurately, it reflects the theoretical difficulties which result from the conceptual elision of men's work with the public, productive sphere, and women's work with the private, reproductive sphere.

The gender, work and class debates comprise the terrain on which much of the research on the gendered division of labour has been conducted, and there are serious problems with some of its key assumptions. The feminist critique has taken two tacks, examining (a) existing ways of including women in the debate; and (b) the premises of class analysis itself as adequate for dealing with social inequality. I will discuss each of these in turn.

2.3.1 Debates within class analysis

Conventional class analysis has taken the male career pattern as typical for purposes of labour market analysis, mobility, and even for deciding what groups will be studied. Goldthorpe (1983, 1984), for instance, dismisses women as peripheral to the study of class structure because their work lives are intermittent, largely part-time, etc. Not only are these assertions empirically questionable, but there is no consideration here of broadening the concept of work altogether. As Abbott and Sapsford (1987: 2) point out, class theorists are quick to suggest that our class imagery is largely formed by our work experiences, yet are content to suggest that wives not employed in the conventional sense (full-time, out of home, continuous, waged labour) derive their sense of political identity and consciousness from their husband's work experience. The debates surrounding gender, work and class have exacerbated the split between the public sphere of work and the private sphere of the household or family. It is what goes on in the former that gives some sort of class position to the latter. Not enough attention has been paid to reciprocal patterns of influence between the two spheres, let alone towards treating the two spheres as co-existing 'moments' in social life. Yet even those attempts to develop new methods of determining women's class position which take women's work into account tend to replicate the elision of work with the public sphere, by focusing on women's *paid* work as what needs to be factored into the class equation. They are still intent on describing a class structure, which exists as a hierarchy of paid occupations, as the primary structure of inequality. That is, gender has become a factor in the question of determining a person's class position, but is not taken as an important dimension of inequality in and of itself. The result has been merely to refine occupational classification schemes to take more adequate account of women's occupational experience (and hence class position) or to develop household ranking procedures, which take the household as a resource-sharing unit with some sort of 'market' or 'life-style' position. In the end, such attempts have tended to become taxonomical exercises which lose sight of the reasons that we should be interested in class analysis in the first place – to understand more clearly the processes and consequences of social inequality.

More fruitful are the feminist approaches which take on class analysis as more fundamentally flawed – that is, they ask whether the concept of class itself, even if some way of measuring women's position within the class structure is found, can be a primary point of reference when seeking to understand the reproduction of social inequality. This has been the important feminist question, and it is on this question that the capitalism versus patriarchy debates have hinged.

2.3.2 Capitalism or patriarchy?

A number of feminist researchers have suggested that class analysis is inadequate as a basis for studying social inequality. Their argument is that class is no more important than other dimensions of inequality – not only gender, but race, ethnicity, sexual orientation and age. Thus, 'a theory which is not able to cope with the articulation of the major sources of social inequality cannot adequately explain inequalities based on only one source, because all sources combine to define social position' (Abbott and Sapsford, 1987: 4). For feminists, gender inequality is not reducible to class inequality.

The studies by Delphy (1984) and Walby (1986) are both extensive critiques of theories which attempt to subsume questions about gender under the more 'important' questions of class. While conventional class theory has looked at men's work in a capitalist mode of production, they recognize as equally (if not more) important, women's work in a patriarchal mode of production – the home.

Delphy (1984: 74) maintains that patriarchy is the 'main enemy' of women. Patriarchy operates through the 'domestic mode of production' (as distinct from the capitalist mode of production). As she analyses it, patriarchal exploitation is the 'common, specific and main oppression of women': common, 'because it affects all married women'; specific 'because only women are under an obligation to perform free domestic services'; and the main form of women's oppression 'because even when women go out to work, the class membership they derive from that work is conditioned by their exploitation as women'. Thus, while she advocates a dual-systems theory of patriarchy and capitalism, her focus is on the former, with relatively little emphasis on the relationship between the two.

Walby (1986) builds on Delphy's work, but stresses the antagonistic relationship between the capitalist mode of production (capitalism) and the domestic mode of production (patriarchy). Challenging the view that capitalism and patriarchy have 'a healthy and strong partnership' (Hartmann, 1981: 19), Walby focuses on the tensions between the two. She defines patriarchy as 'a system of interrelated social structures through which men exploit women' (p. 51) and suggests that the key sets of patriarchal relations are to be found in domestic work, paid work, the state and male violence and sexuality. While the organization of domestic work is characterized as a 'patriarchal mode of production' that is particularly significant in creating gender inequality, 'when patriarchy is in articulation with the capitalist rather than other modes of production, then patriarchal relations in paid work are of central importance to the maintenance of the system' (p. 50). The resulting picture is one of patriarchy and capitalism as independent but articulated systems, in 'considerable antagonism and rivalry over the exploitation of women's labour' (p. 247). The success of men in excluding women from the 'better forms of work' in the labour market creates a situation where 'housework is as good as anything else a woman is likely to get' (p. 248). While Walby's analysis draws much-needed attention to the extent to which patriarchal relations permeate the paid labour market, there are some serious problems with her framework. Biological reproduction and the deeply entrenched assumptions about the 'naturalness' of the relationship between child-bearing, child-rearing and domestic work are barely mentioned – domestic labour under capitalism is something women seem to fall into for lack of opportunity to do anything else. And, like most dual-systems theories, a 'domestic mode of production' exists which stands outside the 'capitalist mode of production'. Once again, the gendered division of labour is taken as coterminous with the public–private division.

Feminist theories of capitalism and patriarchy, while problematic, have greatly advanced our understanding of the arbitrary nature of the division between public and private labour. In summary, it becomes necessary to take, in the tradition of socialist theory, labour as a key category of analysis, but in a much broader sense than it is usually given in the literature. Waged labour is only a portion of the total social labour performed in any society, and the wages – which determine whether labour is public/production or private/reproduction – attached (or not attached) to any particular form of labour are heavily laden with assumptions about what is just, fair and moral. Gender divisions are crucial to all aspects of the social division of labour, and shape both the material and ideological form that those divisions take. What emerges as significant is not so much the physical separation of the public and the domestic, but their ideological separation – that is their separation as realms of thought and experience – and the processes which legitimate this separation. It is increasingly apparent that we cannot view 'the production of things' and the 'production of life' as distinct modes of production, but must see them as integral moments in any mode of production. The public–private division set up as the expression of the gendered division of labour must necessarily fall.

2.4   Rethinking 'Public' and 'Private'

A division of labour by sex and a division between public and private spheres are not identical phenomena. Each has a history, and while one division may be manifest as a crucial form of the other, it is the relationship between the two that is of interest. Thus we need to examine the gendered division of labour and the public versus domestic division as having intertwined, yet separate, trajectories. That is, we cannot neglect the extent to which the sexual division of labour exists within and between each sphere, and the different way in which the gendered division of labour and the public–private dualism have developed historically. As Dorothy Smith (1985: 2) points out, 'It is only in capitalism that we find an economic process constituted independently of the daily and generational production of the lives of particular individuals and *in which therefore we can think economy apart from gender*' [emphasis in the original]. In locating the gendered division of labour as primarily one rooted in this public–private split, 'we are reading back into history. . .a state of affairs peculiar to our own'. As Valverde and Weir (1988) suggest, 'it might be better to look at the ways in which a specific public–private distinction came to be gendered than to make generalizations about women's confinement to privacy'.

In theories of modernity, the notion of kinship has become ambiguous. The concepts of 'household', 'kinship' and 'family', often used interchangeably, are employed to describe important facets of social organization. While seen as varying in importance as organizing principles at various historical junctures, they are also seen as increasingly outside society in the modernization process. The institution of the family has been accorded important status as a moral regulator, socializer, reproducer or 'haven' in a disenchanted world, but it has never been sufficiently deconstructed. It is not enough to examine the institution of kinship or family in relationship to other institutions. We must deconstruct this paradigmatic example of the private sphere into its gendered components, for it is only in this context that the separation of public and private, or of politics, economy and family, makes sense to the project of modernity. As Anderson (1987: 124) suggests in her study of pre-capitalist social organization among the Huron, we need to understand the ways in which 'the gender specific division of labour first separates men from women and the ways in which the kinship structure reunites them into economic, political and familial units'. With the emergence of capitalism, a more detailed analysis of the appearance of kinship as expressed through the 'household' is required. As Rapp (1982: 179) stresses, households and families must be distinguished in order to see 'households as material relations and the family as normative recruitment to those relations'. The economic, political and ideological moments of kinship must be historically examined, to reclaim the family and women's assignment therein from the realm of the natural.

Two tasks seem particularly important here: first, to map out the complex, bi-directional relationships between the domestic and economic spheres in terms of their gender-specific expressions, and second, to indicate the variability of those relationships in specific historical circumstances. Too often, broad statements are made about the effects of capitalist development on the family, neglecting the unevenness that development in different national contexts may bring and suggesting that economic change and changes in domestic arrangements occur in lock-step fashion. While some broad brushstrokes may be drawn, empirical studies continue to demonstrate a wide variability of family forms and relationships in different historical, national and political environments. The theoretical point that becomes clear in all contexts, however, is that 'social formations reproduce themselves in family formations. Cultural norms and material forces are in constant tension; hence any explanation which seeks to appreciate the organization of reproduction must include at its centre an understanding of the relations of production as they influence not only social classes but also men and women' (Levine, 1989: 91).

Work by social historians in Britain (Harris, 1983; Laslett and Wall, 1972; Macfarlane, 1978) has challenged the popular inference that it was industrialization which broke down the extended family into smaller 'nuclear' units. Evidence now suggests that industrialization had less effect on household size than previously thought, and that the nuclear household as the dominant form of organizing domestic life emerged long before, and hence may have had considerable influence upon, the growth of industrialized capitalism. A similar pattern is noted in other industrial countries. Coontz (1988), writing on the United States, and Matthews (1984), summarizing the Australian case, note that European colonists imported with them a nuclear household-family system. Nett (1981), in a useful review of Canadian research, debunks a number of myths about the family. While there was some variation between English and French Canada, with the latter showing higher incidence of extended kin networks, 'it can be said with a fair degree of certainty that the type of household in which most Canadians resided, from the time of settlement in Acadia, New France, New England and later Upper Canada, was the nuclear, or "simple" family' (p. 242). While household structures varied according to stage in the life cycle and economic circumstances, 'the two generation family household was the norm for most colonists and pioneers' (p. 242). Research by Bradbury (1984), Coontz (1988), Gaffield (1984), Katz (1982), Tilly and Scott (1978, 2/1989) and others suggests that among the unskilled urban working class, young couples frequently shared households not with kin, but with unrelated families or couples out of economic necessity. Households also often contained non-family members such as servants and lodgers. Whether households contained members unrelated by kinship or not, they tended to be organized as discrete nuclear 'units'.

Establishing the pre-industrial existence of a household economy, organized around the nuclear family and differentiated by gender, age and kinship is important in its implications for the development of capitalism. Women's labour in subsistence was critical for capital accumulation: 'In the areas characterized by capitalistic productive relations, the existence of family subsistence production prevented wages from rising too rapidly. In the family economy women's subsistence production reduced the need to provide for the family with income from market activities and thus permitted capital to accumulate at a higher rate' (Cohen, 1987: 154).

Women's labour in industrializing societies was, of course, not limited to subsistence production. In North America, Indian women played a crucial role in the fur trade, not only by their labour, which provided traders with the food and clothing essential to their expeditions, but through cementing, via marriage, the commercial and social ties between white traders and native communities that were essential to the fur trade (Brown, 1980; Van Kirk, 1986). Prairie women 'performed whatever work was needed' — be it as independent farmers, farm 'wives', waged workers, entrepreneurs or midwives (Sundberg, 1986). So essential was their labour to the settling of the prairies that unmarried women were actively recruited to the west, through 'emigration societies'. In maritime communities in Europe and North America, women's labour was central to family fishing concerns. In most countries, fishing was in fact 'work for the whole family' (Bradley, 1989: 93). Ephraim Tucker, an American observer in Labrador in 1838, gave the following account: 'When the salmon and trout fishing commences, the women and children employ themselves assiduously in the sport, and are often out night and day while the season of this fishery lasts. At the fish stands, while the cod fishery is in the full tide of operation, the women are seen among the most constant and dexterous in dressing the fish, thrown up by the fishermen. Some of these females will dress two or three thousand fish in a single day' (cited in Prentice et al., 1988: 78). Even after the advent of the 'fish plant', which supplanted the family production unit, women's labour remains vital to 'shore work' in the fishing industry (Bradley, 1989; Connelly and MacDonald, 1986; Porter, 1985).

In rapidly industrializing urban areas, women undertook various types of waged labour outside the home. While domestic service remained a major form of women's employment, throughout the second half of the nineteenth century and the early part of the twentieth, women increasingly took on paid jobs in manufacturing, clerical work, teaching and nursing. By the early twentieth century, employers had come to anticipate and depend on the availability of cheap female labour (Strong-Boag, 1988: 43). Women also took in boarders, did laundry and sewing and produced such commodities as woven goods, wool, butter, cheese and eggs for market distribution, both in urban and rural settings (Bradbury, 1984; Bradley, 1989; Cohen, 1987; Prentice et al., 1988; Tilly and Scott, 1978, 2/1989). Tilly and Scott (1978, 2/1989: 125) cite research on Irish families in nineteenth-century London showing a dramatic increase in boarders in households with young children when the mothers withdrew from the waged labour force. Women played a vital role in industrializing economies; to view this role as solely geared to 'subsistence' or to portray women as 'helpmates' to commodity-producing husbands is to distort both the range and the importance of their labour to economic development. The labour of women and children has always been essential to family survival. With industrialization and the growth in waged labour, the needs of the family economy still dictated the terms under which waged labour would be undertaken – for example, children would go out to work only if their labour could be spared by the household (Conrad, 1986; Tilly and Scott, 1978, 2/1989).

The labour of women in the context of a family economy, whatever form it may have taken, was crucial to the development of capitalism. Yet equally important to remember is that the 'family' owned neither the 'means of production' of the family economy, nor the fruits of its labour – the male head of the household did. Thus, 'the question of power through property relations in general is not unique to capitalist relations, but is crucial to understanding productive relations within the family economy as well' (Cohen, 1987: 44). The 'modern' bourgeois family emerged not with some abstract separation of household and work-place, but with the entrenchment of motherhood as a vocation for white, middle class women. The physical tasks of motherhood declined greatly as these women spent a smaller proportion of their lifespan pregnant and nursing, but the psychological tasks increased (Rapp, 1979: 182). Children had spirits which needed to be properly nurtured, not broken, and it was the mother who was charged with this task: 'By providing the correct environment for child development, mothers undertook the moral regulation of children. The house became an enclosed space, set apart from the outside world, in which this synthetic and controlled environment was created' (Mandell, 1988: 70). A growing social reform movement reinforced women's domestic 'calling' as indispensable to the future of the nation – it was the special qualities of women as mothers that formed a major plank for the suffrage movement. Domestic science became the preferred educational option for girls, preparing them to undertake their future role as guardians of the home. Maternal feminists valorized the mother–child relationship, and undertook to 'educate' working-class mothers, whose economic activities and ignorance of 'scientific' child-rearing techniques were linked to a host of social ills – infant mortality, juvenile delinquency and street gangs, to name a few (Mandell, 1988: 70). The racism of this construction of the 'modern' family is apparent. As Glenn (1991: 193) reminds us, 'a definition of womanhood exclusively in terms of domesticity never applied to racial ethnic women. . . .[T]he maternal and reproductive roles of racial ethnic women were ignored in favour of their roles as workers. The lack of consideration for their domestic functions is poignantly revealed in the testimony of black domestics. . .who were expected to leave their children and home cares behind while devoting full time to the care of the white employer's home and family.'

The solidification of kinship and domesticity in the 'privatized' nuclear family had consequences for men as well. As traditional patriarchal authority gradually waned with the emergence of 'affective individualism' in the family (Stone, 1977) and further state-imposed limits on men's control of women and children, masculinity and male authority came to be defined through the language of 'economic individualism'. As women became constructed in a moral relationship to children and family as the guardians of the family unit, men became defined in an economic relationship as the provider for that unit. The growing administrative state actively regulated these race and gender-specific 'identities' that emerged. The regulation of women's labour and principles for wage-setting both assumed and reinforced the legitimacy of women as mothers who were supported by men as workers.

Corrigan and Sayer (1985: 140–1) note the 1833 Factory Act in England which enshrined age and gender categories into labour regulation: 'The labour force is hence forth split between: children; young persons and women; and adult men. The first category have to be protected. . .; the second category have to be regulated; only the third group are capable of making "free" contracts.'

A similar categorization of labour is found in other countries. Women have always been, and continue to be, constructed as a special category of labour. For example, protective labour legislation often 'had more to do with women as reproducers than with women as wage workers' (Ursel, 1986: 168). Protective legislation regulated the supply and conditions of female and child labour according to what was proper as interpreted by men. In Britain, male unionists testifying to the 1889 Select Committee of the House of Lords on the Sweating System argued for the restriction of women's work because it placed them in direct competition with male workers. The Commissioners, however, 'were more anxious about the immorality of men and women working alongside each other and the dangers working mothers posed to the welfare of the human race' (Lewis, 1986: 104). In Canada, when the Royal Commission on Bell Canada in 1907 found female workers to be horrifyingly exploited, reform was justified not in terms of regulating capital, but by reference to the state's interest in 'regulating the health of young women' (Valverde and Weir, 1988: 32). Similarly, Matthews (1984: 61) summarizes protective legislation in Australia as considering 'all women as potential or actual mothers, nothing more'. Male labour market segments became defined in terms of skill requirements, women's in terms of their 'suitability' to feminine temperament.[4]

Studies of wage and cost of living figures clearly indicate that it was nearly impossible for a female industrial or clerical worker to earn a living wage (Lowe, 1987; Tilly and Scott, 1978, 2/1989; Ursel, 1986). For example, in 1918 the first minimum wage to be implemented in British Columbia, Canada, was largely the result of fears that women would turn to prostitution and crime because they could not live on such low wages.

The whole idea of the 'wage' and its distribution, particularly as it has appeared in discussions of the 'family wage' and the 'family project', deserves closer examination. For much socialist-feminist theory, the idea of the 'family wage' represents a key point of convergence between capitalism and patriarchy. As Sokoloff (1980: 168) summarizes it: 'It was only with the development of the family wage that it was possible for men to be paid a wage that was supposed to be sufficient to reproduce their labour power through the consumption/reproduction work of their wives. . . .It was through the family wage that conflicts between patriarchy and capitalism were resolved and thereby can be said to have cemented the identity of women and nature and her "natural" role in the family.'

Analysis of the wage is placed within the context of a 'family project' as a kinship-based household which pools resources to maximize its potential for survival. These resources include both waged and unwaged labour. Thus, the family/household becomes the intersection of the public and private worlds. Yet a number of key points remain unanalysed in this formulation.

First of all, wages, and the 'family wage' in particular, are overlaid with moral and ideological conceptions about both class and gender. The notion of a 'just price' for labour has always rested on subjective judgements about the morality of social hierarchies: 'It corresponded to a reasonable charge that would enable the producer to support his family on a scale suitable to his station in life' (de Roover, cited in Kessler-Harris, 1988: 239). Most states endorsed a number of principles for the establishment of wages which were explicitly premised on the norm of the male breadwinner. Matthews (1984: 60) cites the Harvester Case of 1907 in Australia which presumed that male workers were supporting families, that female workers had only themselves to support and that paid work for women was an 'interlude before permanent domestic work when women would be "kept" by their husbands for whom public work was a life-long activity'. One of the principles established for the setting of wages in Canada in 1918 reads: 'That all workers, including common labourers, shall be entitled to a wage ample to enable them with thrift to maintain themselves and their families in decency and comfort' (cited in Lewis, 1988: 22). That the worker was a male worker was taken for granted – a corresponding principle stated that only women doing work ordinarily performed by men were entitled to equal pay. Thus, proper social distinctions between classes (with those occupying certain 'stations in life' obviously needing to exercise more 'thrift') and genders, have always permeated the very notion of what constituted a just wage.

Secondly, the family wage is primarily an ideological construction which has never been realized for most of the working class. Women (and children) have long engaged in economic activity to supplement family income in the absence of a family wage. While it is commonly assumed that the growth of waged labour supplanted the family economy, evidence from both historical and current research suggests that the transition has never been complete.[5] Katz (1982: 310) emphasizes the fallaciousness of stressing the separation of family and economy in the process of industrialization, suggesting that 'families always have an economy whether or not all members are engaged in the production of food, commodities or wages'. What is apparent is that the economic contributions of women have never been fully reckoned into the social accounting of productive labour. As Strong-Boag (1988: 41) summarizes it: 'Women's responsibility for housework and child care, coupled with the reality of female wage rates, which were regularly only forty to sixty percent of those paid for comparable male labour, meant that women who wanted to add to the family income were most likely to take on tasks, such as sewing, baby-minding, and taking in boarders, that could be performed at home and that did not require hiring domestic substitutes. Rarely, if ever, were such money-making activities acknowledged in the census. Only the very poor re-entered wage labour as mature women.'

Thirdly, the 'family project' needs to be deconstructed into its gendered components. As a number of writers have pointed out, taking the family unit as the basis of households detracts attention from social relations *within* the household, based on gender, age and kinship statuses, and how these are articulated with the realm of paid employment. Just as in the labour market, the division of labour and the rewards received in families depends more upon the status of the family member than on the nature of the work done or on any measure of ability or need. Families, or households, have never been unproblematic 'units' — they represent a complex of relationships of status, responsibility, power and sexuality based on age, gender and kinship status. It is a mistake to see the family or household as structuring productive relationships only in pre-industrial, pre-capitalist social formations. Labour market participation rates for men and women show that marital status, the stage of family life cycle, age and number of children are related to different expectations about participation in waged labour for both sexes. Not surprisingly, we see male labour-force participation increase at the same point in the life span that women's decreases. The highest participation rate tends to be for married men with pre-school children, the same family situation which results in a low participation rate for women.

While the nuclear family household is clearly not a capitalist invention, the emergence of the modern nuclear family, as it is ideologically constructed around the mother–child nexus, can be considered a mid-nineteenth-century development. It is in these terms that we can understand the distinction between the nuclear household and the nuclear family: while the former appears to have been instrumental as a family economy (often incorporating non-family members) in providing the conditions for capitalist accumulation, the latter evolved to lay the basis for the normative recruitment and structuring of family households in industrialized settings. Viewed in this way, it becomes clear that many accounts of 'modernization' and the family have rested upon rather abstract characterizations of family change, and have periodized history solely from a male, white and ruling-class perspective. The relationship between industrialization and family change was mediated by both race and class.

What directions does this brief review of economic and family change suggest for the theorization of gender in the process of modernity? No natural divisions can be drawn between family, economy and state in the development of gendered spheres. The pre-industrial family economy provided antecedent hierarchies of gender and age, and these both shaped and were shaped by the emerging wage economy and administrative state. As Cohen (1987: 158) summarizes it: 'Not only did new forms of production grow out of old ones, but the very way in which productive relationships changed over time were integrally bound to gendered responses to change'. Nicholson (1986) suggests that it was the unification of kinship with domesticity, associated with the emergence of the modern Western family, that became expressed as the distinction between the 'public' and the 'private'. This leads to the following thesis: that some of the basic categories traditionally employed to explain social life – family, state, economy – reflect historical, and not natural, social divisions. The separation of the family from the state, and the separation of the family from the economy, were (are) historical processes. Thus:

> an analysis which focuses on the historical separation of the economic from the familial enables us to see both the economic nature of gender relations within the family and the gendered aspect of economic relations outside it as a consequence of the emergence of the economy out of kinship' (Nicholson, 1986: 126).

This forces a reconsideration of the accepted theorization of domestic or 'personal' life. Failure to comprehend the crucial role of gender in structuring both public and private life, and the multi-faceted divisions between spheres, has resulted in a reification of the economic individualism of the market. The assumption that kinship and gender were important principles of social organization *only* in pre-industrial, pre-capitalist formations allows only a partial understanding of the complex relationship between kinship, economy and state, and renders a truly sociological analysis of the gendered division of labour, expressed through closely regulated gendered identities, impossible.

To summarize, a division of labour between men and women, and sexual inequality, long pre-date capitalism and have influenced its development. The historical record shows that the nuclear household long pre-dates industrialization and capitalism, and what emerged in conjunction with those developments was the kinship-based family as normative recruitment to households. The historical evidence suggests that gender hierarchies entrenched in household economies were crucial to the birth of capitalism. As Connell (1987: 104) puts it: 'Capitalism was partly constituted out of the opportunities for power and profit created by gender relations. It continues to be.' We need thus to think in terms of a 'gendered logic of accumulation' to refer to the 'gender- structured system of production, consumption and distribution' which 'concentrates economic benefits in one direction, and economic losses in another' (Connell, 1987: 103–5). If we conceive of the development of capitalism in such a way – that is, recognizing not only that there is a logic of accumulation, but that it is from its beginnings a gendered logic – we can move beyond the tenacious account of capitalism simply taking over the pre-existing patriarchal organization of domestic life to use for its own purposes – most commonly phrased in terms of its 'reproduction'. If we rethink the manner in which the gendered division of labour has grounded our understanding of the public–private split, it becomes clear that we need to rethink key parts of our theoretical heritage. The conceptual framework which, whether explicitly or implicitly, has provided the foundation for much socialist feminist theorizing is what I will call the 'reproduction problematic'. The next chapter will examine the concept of social reproduction in relation to the development of socialist feminist theory.

3
Social Reproduction and Socialist Feminist Theory

It should be clear by now that the gendered division of labour is not a remnant of pre-capitalist social organization which capitalism took over and used for its own purposes (i.e. its 'reproduction'). It is actively created and re-created in both 'public' and 'private'. The duality of woman/domestic/private and man/political/public rests upon assumptions which do not stand up to critical examination, and its investigation requires reassessment of the view of 'modernity' that underlies much of our theoretical heritage. I want to turn now to a closer examination of some problems within socialist feminist theory. In particular, I want to look at how 'social reproduction' as a theoretical orientation has been central to the feminist critique.

The concept of 'social reproduction' has a long and uneven history in the literature. With its origins in Marxist class theory, it has often been invoked as an explanatory tool, referring to the complex of social relations and institutions that serve to reproduce capitalism. Rooted in the Hegelian notion of society as a totality, socialist theory has long been concerned with unravelling the relationships among the components of capitalist social formations that secure their continuation. Socialist feminist theories have insisted that not only capitalism, but patriarchy is reproduced; not only is the working class reproduced, but it is reproduced as male and female.

Feminism has not posed the only challenge to an orthodox Marxist conception of social reproduction – in fact, in most accounts, feminist critiques have been ignored or, at best, treated as marginal to mainstream Marxist debates. Debates, such as those concerning the analytical primacy of the mode of production, the autonomy of the political and ideological, and the tension between economism and voluntarism, have fuelled the development of a range of socialist theories which have substantially reconstructed the Marxian problematic. While gender has never been a focus in much of this work, the insights of feminist theory are important to key debates, and the questions raised in these debates are important to feminism. The growth and fragmentation of both Western Marxism in general and socialist feminism in particular have entailed several significant shifts in the 'reproduction problematic'. At each turn, not only valuable insights but unresolved problems have been generated, and this chapter will examine these. I will first sketch the problematic of social reproduction as it has appeared in the literature of Marx and Marxism, through to its explicit abandonment in emergent forms of post-Marxism and poststructuralism. I will then review the manner in which the question of social reproduction has been framed by socialist feminist theories, stressing both their tendency to recycle some of the major flaws of non-feminist theories and the insights they have generated which hold some potential for reconstructing socialist theory. Finally, I will outline some key problems that must be confronted in developing a critical feminist theory which neither dispenses with the insights of reproduction theories nor replicates their most serious errors. Chief among these problems is the failure of most reproduction theories to adequately theorize the subject, thus returning us to some of the basic questions about the individual–society relationship. The importance of theorizing, in an inclusive manner, the production and reproduction of subject-positions is given increased urgency by anti-racist and post-colonial critiques, which further burst open the classical conception of 'modernity' and its analytical categories.

3.1   The Reproduction Problematic in Socialist Theory

3.1.1   Marx and Engels

It is in Marx's theory of history that the seeds of his theory of social reproduction are found. History, for Marx, is the continual process of human beings creating, satisfying and re-creating their needs. In *The German Ideology* he sets out the basics of this historical process as having three 'moments': the satisfaction of basic needs; the simultaneous creation of new needs; and production of new human beings. Yet it is not humans acting in isolation that engage in these historical acts – production is from the outset a social act. 'By social we understand the co-operation of several individuals, no matter under what conditions, in what manner and to what end' (Marx and Engels, 1845–6/1970: 50). Social reproduction, then, must necessarily be the reproduction of social relationships. While Marx at the outset recognized production of 'fresh life in procreation' as one of the 'moments' of production, it was the social relations of material production that occupied the bulk of his subsequent analysis. In his analysis of capitalism, the relationship between capital and wage was the central issue.

In its simplest form, capitalist social reproduction for Marx involved the reproduction of the separation between capital and waged labour through the capitalist production process: 'Capitalist production, therefore, under its aspect of a continuous connected process, of a process of reproduction, produces not only commodities, not only surplus-value, but it also produces and reproduces the capital relation; on the one side the capitalist, on the other the wage-labourer' (Marx, 1867/1946: 591).

'Simple' reproduction is premised upon the appropriation of surplus value by the capitalist class which effectively reproduces the structure of capitalism as is. 'Extended' reproduction implies accumulation, which expands the scale of production and thus transforms the structure somewhat, but in a consistent direction still based on the separation of capital and labour. It was thus the continuity of capitalist production that was the central concern.

Marx himself had little to say about women, as his analysis was largely constructed on an assumption of the worker as the male head of a household. We thus find references to women and children as 'wives and daughters of the proletariat' (Marx and Engels, 1848/ 1948: 27). Engels (1884/1972) replicates Marx's basic assumptions, but was more explicit about the position of women, linking the emergence of the family as an economic unit, monogamous marriage and the dependence of women on men as crucial components of the conditions for the reproduction of the ownership of private property, and hence the capital–wage relationship. Engels (1884/1972: 71) reiterates the central place given to human reproduction in *The German Ideology* in the preface to *Origin of the Family, Private Property and the State*:

> According to the materialist conception, the determining factor in history is, in the final instance, the production and reproduction of immediate life. This, again, is of a twofold character: on the one side, the production of the means of existence, of food, clothing and shelter, and the tools necessary for that production; on the other side, the production of human beings themselves, the propagation of the species.

A number of sympathetic critics have suggested that this passage has often been misinterpreted to legitimize a theoretical separation between human and material reproduction. More correctly, Engels's identification of human reproduction as analytically equivalent to material production sets the basis for his analysis, but he is unsuccessful in maintaining this in its execution. Human reproduction 'slips' in status: 'As human reproduction slides out of the material base, its organization becomes dependent on the organization of production' (Humphries, 1987: 11). We are thus returned to the organization of material production, and specifically capitalist relations of material production, as pre-eminent in the theory of social reproduction.

For classical Marxist theory, then, society is a totality – an historically produced whole, whose most fundamental relationships are production relations. As Marx summarizes it:

> This conception of history depends on our ability to expound the real process of production, starting out from the material production of life itself, and to comprehend the form of intercourse connected with this and created by this mode of production (i.e. civil society in

its various stages), as the basis of all history; and to show it in its action as State, to explain all the different theoretical products and forms of consciousness, religion, philosophy, ethics, etc. etc. and trace their origins and growth from that basis; by which means, of course, the whole thing can be depicted in its totality (and therefore, too, the reciprocal action of these various sides on one another) (Marx and Engels, 1845–6/1970: 58).

The whole question of the individual–society relationship turns on labour as the constitutive human activity, and productive relations as framing political society. Individuals are the carriers of abstract, historically produced relations – they are 'the personifications of economic categories, embodiments of particular class-relations and class interests' (Marx, 1867/1946: 21). This renders, for Marx at least, questions of identity and agency relatively unproblematic. These questions, however, become key points of contention as Marx's understanding of social reproduction has been challenged by those involved in subsequent Marxist theory, feminist theory and other emancipatory discourses.

3.1.2   The fragmentation of Western Marxism

To speak of Marx is one thing – to speak of Marxism is quite another. Marxism, as Smart (1992: 208) notes, has 'been in crisis almost from its inception. . . .The history of Marxism is punc-tuated with crucial debates, turning points, repeated calls for clarification and revision, as well as reinterpretations and reformula-tions following critical reflections on changes in socioeconomic circumstances and developments in theory and analysis'. For example, the Hegelian Marxism of Georg Lukács and Karl Korsch, Antonio Gramsci's 'philosophy of praxis' and the 'critical theory' of the Frankfurt School all represented attempts to develop Marxism in response to twentieth-century conditions – in particular, the emergence of bureaucratic socialism in Eastern Europe and the tenacity of capitalism in Western Europe and North America. It is significant to note that the concept of social reproduction in Western Marxism 'has become prominent in the past two decades primarily in the context of the analysis of superstructural phenomena', and has led to increased interest in processes of *cultural* reproduction (Morrow and Torres, 1987: 22). Close examination of the complex issues underlying the fragmentation of contemporary Marxism is beyond the scope of this chapter.[1] Nonetheless, a summary of the central differences in approaches to the problem of social reproduction as they have emerged in the last few decades is warranted.

In the development of Western Marxism, theories have tended to cluster around two poles, each emphasizing different themes in Marx's work. Gouldner (1983) refers to the 'two Marxisms' as scientific and humanist; Howard (1977) speaks of 'materialist' and 'idealist' strains; and Hall (1980) refers to the 'two paradigms' of structuralism and culturalism. As Hall (1981: 381) points out, both approaches developed in reaction to 'economism' – the reductionist interpretation of the base–superstructure metaphor into which political Marxism congealed in the early twentieth century.

The work of Althusser is generally seen as the exemplar of a structuralist reading of Marx. Althusser explicitly reframed the Marxist base–superstructure distinction in terms of social reproduction. Seeing society as a complex, structured totality, he argued that the political and ideological levels were not merely reflections of the economic level, but rather had 'relative autonomy'. Borrowing the psychoanalytic concept of 'overdetermination' to understand the complex and shifting relationships between the economic and ideological levels, he nonetheless saw the economic level as determinate in 'the last instance'. Yet ideology and 'ideological state apparatuses' were accorded an important place in the overall process of social reproduction. That is, capitalism depends not only on the continued reproduction of the forces of production (the means of production and labour power), but also of the relations of production (the social organization of production based on ownership and control of the forces of production). The latter requirement is accomplished by ideological state apparatuses, such as the educational system, the family and the media. The import of Althusser's work lies in his conception of the production of ideology as being as crucial to the reproduction of capitalist societies as the production of goods. 'Ideology' is not simply a distorted reflection of material reality, or a cloak which prevents us from seeing how things really work – it is integral to the production of subjects.[2] Althusser's analysis emphasizes the manner in which we live ideology — actual agency is an illusion:

> The structure of the relations of production determines the places and functions occupied and adopted by the agents of production, who are never anything more than the occupants of these places. . . .The true 'subjects' (in the sense of constitutive subjects of the process) are therefore not these occupants or functionaries. . .but the definition and distribution of these places and functions (Althusser and Balibar, 1965/1970: 180)

Craib (1984: 144) aptly uses the metaphor of the puppet theatre to describe this conception of the subject: 'the strings originate at the economic level, the mode of production; they pass through the state and the ideological state apparatuses. . .and they finally work the puppets through an imaginary sense of being free, of choosing, of acting'. It is not difficult to see the underlying functionalism of this approach. All the parts of the structure are theorized in terms of the function they perform in reproducing that structure, and 'subjects' are inextricably dominated by that structure. The important criticisms of this approach are those directed at its ahistorical nature — the relatively static model of society upon which it depends — and the problem of subjectivity. If subjectivity is an illusion, what are the possibilities for liberating the puppets? As Connell (1979) suggests in his cogent critique of the Althusserian approach to class, the political import of this is an implicit defence of a quasi-Stalinist revolutionary vanguard as the only route towards transformation.

The influence of Althusser remains visible in a number of more recent Marxist approaches to social reproduction. The introductions to two anthologies purporting to deal with the question of social reproduction in advanced capitalist societies illustrate this. Walker (1978: xiii) defines social reproduction as 'all the various social relations and institutions that serve to reproduce society without any fundamental change', and lists as its main aspects the technical division of labour in the firm, the social division of labour in society, the educational system, the state and the family. Dickinson and Russell (1986: 5) define social reproduction as an approach which 'takes the dominant relationship of our time — the wage labour/capital relationship — as its principal object of analysis and considers the institutions, mechanisms and processes associated with the economic, social, political and ideological reproduction of this relationship'. Thus, while the analysis takes in a number of different factors outside the economy, there is an invariant structure (the capital–wage relationship) which is posited as being reproduced in an explicitly functionalist fashion. What was 'equilibrium' or 'pattern maintenance' in functionalism becomes 'social reproduction' in structuralist Marxism. As Willis (1981b: 52) sums it up: 'With no sense of structure being a contested medium as well as an outcome of social process, "Reproduction" becomes a mechanized sleight of hand in an oh so serious theoretical vaudeville!'

While structuralism builds on the second half of Marx's famous pronouncement on history – that we make our own history, but not under conditions of our choosing – cultural Marxism emphasizes the first half. The shift in attention from structure to agency is accompanied by an epistemological shift to hermeneutic and historical methodology. While the culturalist approach lacks a dominant exponent such as Althusser, it draws on the work of such diverse figures as Lukács, Gramsci, Raymond Williams and E.P. Thompson.

Gramsci, for example, takes economic reductionist versions of Marxism to task for their 'deterministic, fatalistic and mechanistic' elements (1929–35/1971: 336). For Gramsci, structures and super-structures comprise an 'historic bloc', within which ideologies provide the form through which we experience material forces. While hegemonic ideologies promote the consent of the oppressed, they are not absolute – there are always spaces for the development of 'political consciousness'. He insists on an historical analysis of ideologies, and one which does not immediately treat anything 'ideological' as negative. As he elaborates it:

> One must therefore distinguish between historically organic ideologies, those, that is, which are necessary to a given structure, and ideologies that are arbitrary, rationalistic, or "willed". To the extent that ideologies are historically necessary they have a validity which is "psychological"; they "organise" human masses, and create the terrain on which men move, acquire consciousness of their position, struggle, etc. (1929–35/1971: 376–7).

Gramsci's analysis of cultural hegemony and historically situated forms of consciousness continues to be influential in culturalist Marxism.

As Hall (1980: 69) suggests, the strengths of culturalism can be derived from the weaknesses of structuralism, and 'from the latter's strategic absences and silences'. While structuralist Marxism stresses the 'power of objective structures of social relations of a particular social formation', culturalists stress the subjective moment — 'the actual lived experience and interpretation of class, race and gender actors' (Apple, 1983: ix). Hall (1980) makes an important distinction between structuralism and culturalism in terms of the focus on 'ideology' in the former, and 'culture' in the latter. Structuralism tended to interpret ideology negatively, as a resource of the dominant class used 'to reproduce the social relations and attitudes needed to sustain the social divisions of labour necessary for the existing relations of production' (Giroux, 1983b: 76). A shift in focus to culture represents an attempt to grasp the complex way in which human practices constitute and are constituted by both ideological and structural moments: 'Culture is the distinctive shapes in which the material and social organization of life expresses itself.. . Culture is the way the social relations of a group are structured and shaped, but it is also the way those shapes are experienced, understood and interpreted' (Hall and Jefferson, 1976: 10). The problematic of social reproduction is pushed beyond the reproduction of the capital–wage relationship.

In addition to the focus on culture versus ideology, the very concepts rejected by Althusserian structuralism — historicism and subjectivity — are those embraced by culturalism. The historical subject becomes the focus of analysis. In opposition to the structuralist interpretation of history as a process without subjects, E.P. Thompson (1978: 296) writes: 'history cannot be compared to a tunnel through which an express races until it brings its freight of passengers out into sunlit plains. Or, if it can be, then generation upon generation of passengers are born, live in the dark, and die while the train is still within the tunnel.' Consciousness and experience become central to any account of historical process. 'Culture' thus takes on the status of a relatively autonomous realm in the social totality, one which is not a correspondence of the economic base, but is constituted by the active practices of living, breathing subjects.

The principal critique of culturalism has been that it valorizes experience and 'meaning', and that this results in a lapse into pure voluntarism. Such writers, as Anderson (1980) charge that without attention to the structural conditions of action, only one side of the dialectic is presented. The culturalist emphasis on experience, and antipathy to causal analyses, also leads to accusations that it is an anti-theoretical stance. Yet the politicization of culture and the strong historical component of the culturalist approach have served as an important corrective to structuralist accounts.

3.1.3 Abandoning the reproduction problematic: poststructuralism

Common to any theory of social reproduction is some notion of society as a totality. Several recent contributions to socialist theory have abandoned the notion of totality altogether, and have thus dissolved the problematic of social reproduction. Illustrative in this respect is work such as that of the loosely knit category of 'poststructuralism', in which I include theorists such as Foucault and Derrida, and that of Laclau and Mouffe (1985) which defines itself as 'post Marxist'. It is a vast oversimplification to group their work together, but in spite of differences there are some common themes. If anything characterizes this theoretical turn, it is a rejection of any notion of social unity or constancy – there is only narrative order which is discursively imposed. Alongside the dissolution of totality is the dissolution of any notion of the coherent subject or unified identity, such as was presumed in classical Marxism's understanding that one's subjectivity was derived from one's place in the productive order.

Foucault has an ambivalent relationship to the Marxist tradition: while he has clearly been influenced by it, he rejects most of its basic analytical categories.[3] In a clear departure from the tradition of historical materialism, he has directed his work against the notion of totality or 'totalization' in history:

> My aim is most decidedly not to use the categories of cultural totalities (whether world-views, ideal types, the particular spirit of the age) in order to impose on history, despite itself, the forms of structural analysis. The series described, the limits fixed, the comparisons and correlations made are based not on the old

philosophies of history, but are intended to question teleologies and totalizations (Foucault, 1969/1972: 15–16).

Against structuralism's adherence to notions of correspondence, it is a doctrine of non-correspondence. There is no continuity to history, no internal relationship between empirical observations which lie in wait for the theorist to discover them. To speak of continuous history is to impose the discourse of the present on the past, and to speak of 'totality' is to suggest political totalitarianism. Foucault's strategy is to unmask totalizing discourse, a category into which most theories of social reproduction must fall, as inherently authoritarian. His concern is to emancipate 'subjugated know-ledges' from this 'coercion' of totalizing theory through a detailed non-economic analysis of power.

> What, must we ask, is this power — or rather, since that is to give a formulation to the question that invites the kind of theoretical coronation of the whole which I am so keen to avoid — what are the various contrivances of power, whose operations extend to such differing levels and sectors of society and are possessed of such manifold ramifications? What are their mechanisms, their effects and their ramifications? (Foucault, 1980: 87–8).

Foucault's work has been enormously influential, and has enriched both the scope and the vocabulary of contemporary theory. He has directed our gaze to the myriad of ways and the multiplicity of sites through which subjection and struggle have constituted history. Yet his refusal of any conception of totality and his reluctance to confront normative questions have political conse-quences. As Poster (1984: 151) sums it up: 'he does not provide a theoretical basis for distinguishing between discourses that lead to domination and those that pave the way for liberation. He never meditates on the power effect of his own discourse or provides criteria by which one can distinguish its conservative and radical modes.' This problem is common to the poststructuralist dissolu-tion of totality more generally.

Laclau and Mouffe (1985) dismiss the Marxist notion of a social totality as 'essentialism', and call for a conception of the social which is 'open' and 'unsutured': 'we must begin by renouncing the conception of "society" as founding totality of its partial processes. . . .There is no sutured space peculiar to "society", since the social itself has no essence' (p. 95–6). Their strategy is to rework the concept of hegemony as a 'logic of the contingent' by deconstructing what they have construed as Marxism's congealment of hegemony into determinacy. They treat the introduction of hegemony into Marxist analysis, particularly via Gramsci, not as a concept which enriched or extended that analysis, but as one which lays the ground for it to be superceded. Mounting an offensive against the association of identity with class position, and of relationships with production, they proceed to burst open the 'subject' as a unitary entity. Instead, they offer a dispersion of 'subject positions' within a 'discursive structure' which is hege-monically (contingently) overdetermined:

> the epistemological niche from which "universal" classes and subjects spoke has been eradicated, and it has been replaced by a polyphony of voices, each of which constructs its own irreducible discursive identity (Laclaus and Mouffe, 1985: 195).

Importantly, 'each of these diverse elements and levels is no longer the expression of a totality which transcends it' (p. 195). What does this mean for the problematic of social reproduction? Essentially, it dissolves the notion altogether – there is no 'society', nothing social to be reproduced. We are left with a plurality of discursively dispersed and 'hegemonically articulated' subject positions, with no concept of social reality to place limits on or inform their action or consciousness. Laclau and Mouffe have produced a provocative critique of Marxist theory, particularly powerful in the doubts they cast on class as the primary determinant of identity and on socialism as the emancipatory end of politics. However, the ensuing political agenda of a 'radical democracy' that they present is problematic. There is no grounding for transformation here (for what is to be transformed?), only the promise of free-floating, discursive, guerilla-style intellectual attacks.

While post-Marxist and poststructuralist critiques have been helpful in exposing some of the excesses of structuralism and subjectivism, the power of social criticism embodied in Marxist theories of social reproduction, and indeed the political import of Marx himself, is jettisoned. The liberatory potential of the con-ception of totality lies in its enabling us to envision a different totality, to theorize transformation rather than reproduction. Without the idea of an historically situated totality which is subject to transformation, we are left with only negative politics. The implication is that 'there can be no way of establishing social or political priorities, and hence no prospect of elaborating a genuinely emancipatory strategy. The result is a political relativism which cannot be progressive' (Wilson and Weir, 1986: 107).

Social reproduction in socialist theory has appeared as both a seemingly powerful explanatory concept and as a fundamental problematic. Underlying conceptions of how society is constituted, and how elemental relationships are reproduced (or whether in fact they are reproduced) have permeated the development and fragmentation of Marxist social theories to the present day. The structuralist–culturalist divide has centred on reproduction as historical law versus reproduction as contingent and experiential. Their different conceptions of totality have resulted in a tendency for both sides to replicate, rather than overcome, the fundamental dualism between agency and structure. Current developments in post-Marxist and poststructuralist theory suggest abandonment of the concept of totality, and hence any notion of social reproduction (or transformation) altogether.

As socialist feminist theory has developed, it has not been immune from these debates. The seductiveness of 'social reproduction' as a way of 'counting women in' resulted in its often uncritical adoption in feminist circles. The analytical force and grand historical sweep of Marxism's categories and frameworks seemed to provide powerful tools for the analysis of women's oppression. However, the inadequacies of an analysis of women's oppression as deriving principally from capitalist productive relationships became quickly apparent as socialist feminist theories flourished. It is to the development of socialist feminist theories on these terms that I now turn.

3.2   The Reproduction Problematic in Socialist Feminist Theory

While Marxist theories of social reproduction were centrally concerned with the reproduction of capitalism, taking class relations as the basic organizing principle of history, the feminist critique insisted that we also need to account for the existence and persistence of sexual inequality. Socialist feminist theory has thus been centrally concerned with the relationship between capitalism and patriarchy, and the reproduction of both class and gender relations. As in Western Marxism generally, there remain a number of contentious theoretical issues in the trajectory of the 'reproduction problematic' in socialist feminist theory.

3.2.1 The domestic labour debates

The domestic labour debates represented a concerted effort by feminists to analyse women's oppression within Marxism. While criticizing Marx for ignoring women's unpaid labour as an important factor in social reproduction, they nonetheless remained relatively faithful to Marx's overall concept of social reproduction, which, again, was primarily concerned with the reproduction of the relationship between capital and labour. Key questions included the value of domestic labour, and the centrality of women's domestic work in reproducing capitalist relations of production. While they served an important role in making women visible in Marxist analyses, the domestic labour debates have been criticized for being overly economistic and functionalist, and as Burton (1985: xvi) notes, for relying on 'a class analysis of categories rather than of relationships'.

What is important for our purposes is not a detailed analysis of the insights and impasses of the work on domestic labour, but rather the premises upon which the debates were conducted. Marx and Engels asserted that the 'production of people' was as important as the 'production of goods', in analytical terms; if this is accepted, there are grounds for treating the 'mode of production' as constituted by both (and for treating 'relations of production' as all those social relations within which production, more broadly conceived, occurs). The domestic labour debates, however, interpreted the mode of production as the production of material goods, and set up human reproduction, and the reproduction of waged labour, as being processes which occur *outside* the mode of production proper. This shift in interpretation was no doubt facilitated because Marx and Engels failed to develop their original insights on human reproduction. As Sayer (1987: 81) suggests:

> Had Marx developed his broader German Ideology view of 'the production of life', the conceptual apparatus of historical materialism might have looked very different. . . .Class relations would remain a central dimension, but would not necessarily be seen as the central – let alone the exclusive – dimension of social structure.

Neither Marx, nor Engels, nor the participants in the domestic labour debates developed historical materialism in this way. The splitting off of the production of goods from the production of people, with the latter being accorded a supporting role in the *reproduction* of the former, laid the basis for more than a decade of debate around the relative priority of capitalism versus patriarchy and class versus gender.

The domestic labour debates served an important purpose in their insistence that gender had something to do with the social division of labour, and that there was a structural basis to women's inequality. Yet as long as the capital–wage relationship is held as the key production relationship, its reproduction will be defined in terms of a narrowly interpreted base–superstructure image, with the production of material goods as the base. Once this basic framework is accepted, it becomes difficult to do anything but describe (but not really explain) how a sexual division of labour 'functions' to reproduce the relations of production thus defined. This was the crucial failure of the domestic labour debates, and one which much subsequent Marxist theory has replicated.

A number of key problems remain for socialist feminist theory in taking up the social reproduction problematic as its own. Not the least of these is the conceptual confusion around the term 'reproduction'. Edholm, Harris and Young (1977), for example, identify three separate interpretations of the concept: social reproduction (the reproduction of the main production relations in society); reproduction of the labour force (socialization and maintenance of workers); and human reproduction (procreation). There has been a distinct lack of success in the literature in developing an adequate theoretical framework based on these often confused interpretations of 'reproduction'. Pahl (1984: 328), for example, distinguishes between biological, cultural (symbolic) and social (material) reproduction, suggesting that they are related, but he dismisses the need for careful examination of their relationship: 'It seems to me to be self-evident that social, cultural and biological reproduction are the central social processes of society and that the household has been the basic instrument for achieving such reproduction at least since the thirteenth century. . .and probably well before that' (pp. 328–9). Such an assertion sweeps a number of important questions regarding the relationship between 'reproductive' processes under the rug, including the question of how individual subjects are caught up in these 'central social processes'.

3.2.2   The Althusserian legacy

Still committed to a Marxist analysis of capitalism, but posing distinctly feminist questions, was the work of feminists influenced by Althusserian Marxism. Most notable in this vein was Juliet Mitchell's *Women's Estate* (1971), in which she set out to 'ask the feminist questions, but try to come up with some Marxist answers' (p. 99). Using the conception of the social formation as a complex structured totality, and the notion of overdetermination, she analysed women's oppression as anchored in four 'structures': production, reproduction, sexuality and socialization. 'In a complex totality each independent sector has its own autonomous reality though each is ultimately, but only ultimately, determined by the economic factor. . .Because the unity of woman's condition at any time is in this way the product of several structures, moving at different paces, it is always "overdetermined" (p. 101). Each of the structures has its own history, each generates its own form of sexual domination, and each can be in contradiction with another; but just as it was for Althusser, the economic factor is the final determinant. With the placement of reproduction, sexuality and socialization beside production in the analysis, women's oppression becomes a much more complex phenomena than the domestic labour debates would suggest. Importantly, women's role in the family, defined as a patriarchal (not just capitalist) configuration, and the family as an ideological apparatus, were implicated in each of these 'structures'.

More recently, structuralist Marxism has been given currency in feminist work by Giminez (1982, 1987). Drawing on both Althusser and the structuralist anthropology of Godelier, she outlines what might be termed a 'correspondence' theory of women's oppression, referring to the elements of the totality as the mode of production and 'its corresponding social, political, legal, and ideological structures' (1987: 54). Chief among these corresponding structures is the family – the context in which social classes are reproduced, and through which the capitalist mode of production 'recruits' men and women for the positions of 'agents of reproduction'. Giminez (1982: 320) summarizes the essence of her argument as follows:

> In capitalist social formations, the observable forms of sexual inequality are determined, in the last instance, by the historically specific way in which the mode of production (conceived as a complex structured whole in which the capitalist mode of production is dominant) affects the access of the labouring and nonlabouring members of the subordinate classes. . .to the material conditions necessary for their daily and generational reproduction.

Social reproduction again becomes the reproduction of classes – if we strip away the abstractions, there is little left but the logic of capital winging its way through history.

As Lieven (1981: 261) suggests, there were two reasons why Althusser's formulation was attractive to feminists. First, he provided a theory of ideology which articulated its autonomous effect, thus opening lines of inquiry around the family, the state, and the educational system as 'apparatuses' implicated in the reproduction of both capitalism and women's oppression. Secondly, he suggested psychoanalytic (specifically Lacanian) concepts as useful tools in understanding the internalization of ideology. As Mitchell (1974) argues, we need to understand how ideology functions through the unconscious, positing the unconscious as 'the domain of the reproduction of culture or ideology' (p. 413). Gimenez is less sanguine about the usefulness of psychoanalytic theory, but concedes that feminist analyses of psychological oppression might be critically appropriated if they are first 'integrated with the Structuralist Marxist analysis of their specifically capitalist structural and superstructural determinants' (1982: 321).

The debates of the late 1970s and early 1980s around the 'unhappy marriage' of Marxism and feminism (Eisenstein, 1979; Sargent, 1981) confronted the problems of the structuralist legacy. Hartmann (1981: 2) took the metaphor of 'a marriage' literally: 'The "marriage" of marxism and feminism has been like the marriage of husband and wife depicted in English common law: marxism and feminism are one, and that one is marxism . . . .Either we need a healthier marriage or we need a divorce.' The solution seemed to be some form of 'dual-systems' theory — the positing of capitalism and patriarchy as separate but related systems of social relations. The problem with this, as Young (1981: 49) suggests, is that it accepts Marxism's 'gender blind analysis of the relations of production, wishing only to add onto it a separate conception of the relations of gender hierarchy'.

3.2.3 *Psychoanalysis and feminism*

After the Second World War there were several divergent attempts to integrate psychoanalytic concepts with Marxist analysis in order to account for the ideological reproduction of workers under capitalism. Feminist theory in the 1970s approached the ideological reproduction of men and women, or more specifically masculinity and femininity, in a similarly diverse fashion. I will briefly outline two such approaches here — those of Juliet Mitchell (1974) and Nancy Chodorow (1978).

Mitchell may be credited with introducing — at least to English-speaking audiences — the utility of psychoanalysis for feminist inquiry. Until the publication of her *Feminism and Psychoanalysis* in 1974, Freud had been denounced by most feminists as justifying women's oppression through a creed of 'biology is destiny'. Mitchell turned this indictment of psychoanalysis back on itself, suggesting that: 'However it may have been used, psychoanalysis is not a recommendation *for* a patriarchal society, but an analysis *of* one' (1974: xiii). Mitchell's appropriation of psychoanalysis builds on a structuralist theory of ideology (influenced by Althusser), and a structuralist theory of kinship (influenced by Levi-Strauss), and it is the relationship she sketches between these two 'structures' and the unconsciousness that has been influential in feminist theory. Setting up the 'economic mode of capitalism and the ideological mode of patriarchy' as 'two autonomous areas', she asserts that 'patriarchal law speaks to and through each person in his [sic] unconscious' (1974: 412–3). Barrett (1980: 61–2) finds this position leading not only to analytical problems, but to limited political ends:

> In particular it tends to the conclusion that class struggle requires economic change, whereas women's liberation requires a 'cultural revolution'. . . .The ideology of masculinity and femininity, of heterosexual familialism, is too deeply embedded in the division of labour and capitalist relations of production to crumble under cultural and ideological offensive alone.

A more sociological account than Mitchell's is given in Chodorow's *The Reproduction of Mothering* (1978). Taking the problematic of social reproduction from the societal to the psychological level, she constructs her theory on the universal fact that it is women who mother. She interprets this not as a biologically given necessity, but as a cultural invention which has become integrated into the feminine psyche. Because women have almost exclusive responsibility for the care of the young, children experience a sexually differentiated process of individuation and separation. Girls experience a lack of separation from the mother, which leads them to want to be mothers. Boys, on the other hand, must learn that they are different. They cannot identify with the femininity of the mother, yet do not have the close proximity to the father (because he is away from the private sphere of the home), so they must turn to the cultural image of masculinity. Influenced by the work of the early Frankfurt School on authority and the family, she thus posits that female-centred child-rearing reproduces not only motherhood, but capitalism, by turning girls into mothers and boys into workers. The reorganization of parenting thus becomes a central political goal. Yet, as Donovan (1985: 112) notes: 'Chodorow seems to think that if people become non-functional to the capitalist work structure, it will wither away.' Furthermore, Tanya Modleski's commentary on the contemporary cultural celebration of fatherhood (illustrated by the spate of such films as *Three Men and a Baby*) cautions that men may respond to the call, implied by Chodorow's analysis, for increased participation in child-rearing 'in such a way as to make women more marginal than ever' (Modleski, 1991: 88).

The chief criticism of these psychoanalytic approaches to the reproduction of sexual inequality relates to its assumption of an ahistorical and transcultural kinship structure as being at the root of women's oppression. To consider women universally as 'mothers' is to deny the complexity and contradictions of the social relations in which women's oppression can be located. Elizabeth Wilson makes a more serious charge – that psychoanalytic feminism becomes an expression of 'psychic law and order', and suggests only 'endless contemplation of how we came to be chained': 'The last thing feminists need is a theory that teaches them only to marvel anew at the constant recreation of the subjective reality of subordination and which reasserts male domination more securely than ever within theoretical discourse' (Wilson, 1986: 168).

In spite of their shortcomings, the initial attempts to theorize the reproduction of masculinity and femininity at the level of individual psyche were important in introducing this level of analysis into socialist feminist theory. It is a level of analysis which continues to be central and one to which I shall return in chapter 4. The theorization of the reproduction of masculinity and femininity is directly related to the problems in classical Marxism of the theorizing subject positions which do not derive solely from the structure of productive relations. One response to these problems in feminism has been a turn to the poststructuralist dissolution of the subject.

3.2.4   *Poststructuralism and feminism*

Two strands of poststructuralist theory have emerged most prominently in the feminist literature: the work associated with French feminists[4] drawing on Lacan's psychoanalysis and Derrida's linguistic deconstruction (Cixous, 1985; Fraser and Bartky, 1992; Irigaray, 1985; Kristeva, 1980, 1981, 1982); and the primarily Anglo-American work influenced by Foucault's version of discourse theory (Butler, 1990; Diamond and Quinby, 1988; Sawicki, 1992; Weedon, 1987).

For Kristeva (1982: 39), sexual difference 'is translated by and translates a difference in the relationship of subjects to the symbolic contract which *is* the social contract; a difference, then, in the relationship to power, language and meaning'. Picking up on Lacan's emphasis on language as the symbolic order of power, women become defined by their exclusion from that order, by what they are *not*. As Irigaray (1985) puts it, we are 'the sex which is not one'. It is not transformation which is our political aim, it is rupture – 'the explosion of social codes' (Kristeva, 1980: 166). To talk of feminism is to invoke only a temporary category of 'speaking subjects'.

More than one writer has suggested that Foucault represents the variety of poststructuralist theory 'which is arguably of most interest to feminists' (Weedon, 1987: 22; see also Fraser, 1992a). Of particular interest has been his theory of discourse and power, and within this theory, his work on the production and control of sexuality. Foucault's conception of power as plural and not entirely negative, and his deconstructive approach to the 'subject', have been instructive for feminists. As Martin (1988: 16) sums it up:

> What is useful for us is the suggestion to be read out of Foucault's work that we analyze the historically and discursively specific ways in which woman has figured as a constitutive absence. To totalize or universalize Otherness as an answer to the question of woman is to leave ourselves with no possibility for understanding or intervening in the processes through which meaning is produced, distributed, and transformed in relation to the shifting articulation of power in our world.

In poststructuralism, the subject becomes decentred and dispersed, constituted in a multiplicity of power relations that produce meanings. While this assists us in grasping sexual oppression in its 'endless variety', it does little for our understanding of its 'monotonous similarity' (Fraser and Nicholson, 1990: 34). The poststructuralist attitude towards subjectivity results in what Alcoff (1988: 417) terms a 'nominalist' conception of woman: 'the idea that the category "woman" is a fiction and that feminist efforts must be directed toward dismantling this fiction'. At face value it holds promise, suggesting the possibility of transcending conceptions of femininity as essential and unchangeable, yet leaves us only with Kristeva's strategy of negative struggle. As Alcoff notes, 'nominalism threatens to wipe out feminism itself'; 'What can we demand in the name of women if "women" do not exist and demands in their name simply reinforce the myth that they do? How can we speak out against sexism as detrimental to the interests of women if the category is a fiction?' (p. 420).

The poststructuralist challenge to essentialist, mechanical theories of social reproduction is one which feminist theory must take, and is taking, seriously. Our task, however, is to incorporate its insights while rejecting its nihilistic tendencies. In particular, given the emancipatory aims of feminism, the subject-structure relationship must be recast to allow for transformative agency.

In sum, socialist feminist approaches to social reproduction have been both fruitful and problematic. Aside from the difficulties with social reproduction theory in general, there has been the more fundamental problem for feminists of attempting to squeeze gender into a model ultimately based on the reproduction of class relations. While the domestic labour debates put women on the Marxist agenda, allegiance to an orthodox interpretation of Marx's political economy closed off a number of important questions, particularly around the relation of women to men. Retaining the primacy of the reproduction of capitalism as determinant in reproducing women's oppression leads to the assumption of a conspiracy between the owners of capital and all men. Structuralist Marxism's location of women's oppression in both an economic base and a relatively autonomous superstructure has generated volumes of insightful and creative work on the four 'structures' outlined by Mitchell, but generally allowed the gender-blind analysis of production to retain primacy, adding on patriarchal relations in some version of 'dual-systems' theory. In spite of the insights into the ideological reproduction of masculinity and femininity provided by the psychoanalytic theory, the resulting picture is one of a relatively universal and unchangeable structuring of both psyche and society with little room for human agency in effecting change. All of these approaches tend to recycle the subject–structure dualism. Poststructuralist interpretations correctly criticize the 'reproductive logic' implied by previous approaches, but abandoning the problematic altogether abandons its political import.

Each approach has uncovered important problems and introduced useful concepts, but each has also generated unresolved problems which are important to social theory in general. It is clear that feminist theory needs to articulate more clearly the role of human agency in both reproducing and transforming structures of domination, and to ground more firmly its insights as a basis for transformation. To do so first requires a more thorough examination of some of the current theoretical impasses.

3.3   Dilemmas in Socialist Feminist Theory

A review of some of the debates within socialist feminist theory over the last decade (Armstrong and Armstrong, 1990; Barrett, 1984; Barrett, 1988a; Brenner and Ramas, 1984; Connelly, 1983; Hansen and Philipson, 1990: Morgen, 1990) illustrates that while consensus has been reached on some issues, others remain contentious. A degree of consensus seems to have been reached on the need to abandon the dual-systems approach, with its positing of capitalism and patriarchy as relatively autonomous, yet mutually supportive and interrelated systems of domination. There appears to be general agreement that analytically separating the ideological and the material is fruitless, and that capitalism and patriarchy are so interwoven as to be one and the same system — 'capitalist patriarchy', as Eisenstein (1979) termed it. Yet while there is agreement on the linkage of capitalism and patriarchy into a seemingly unitary system of domination, integrated through the sexual division of labour, three key issues seem to dominate current debates: (a) the level at which the interrelationship of capitalism and patriarchy is most appropriately theorized; (b) the relative weighting that should be accorded to material and ideological factors; and (c) the charge that socialist feminist theories have marginalized race and ethnicity.

The first debate revolves around the level of analysis at which the sexual division of labour is essential to the reproduction of capitalism. The interpretation most faithful to an orthodox base—superstructure metaphor sees the insertion of a sexual division of labour as necessary at the most abstract level of analysis. For example, Armstrong and Armstrong (1983: 39) argue that 'because capitalism is premised on free wage labour — on the separation of most aspects of workers' reproduction from the production process — women's reproductive capacities separate them out of the production process for child-bearing work. This establishes the basis for an elaboration of sex differences, a sexual division of labour which subordinates women and pervades all levels of human activity under capitalism.' While I think that Armstrong and Armstrong are correct to insist that the sexual division of labour is integral to the capitalist mode of production, they seem to neglect that concepts such as 'the capitalist mode of production' or the 'sexual division of labour' do not exist *per se*. They are abstractions of principles from the level of historically situated, concrete social formations. Others, such as Jenson (1986), Omvedt (1986), Riley (1983) and Walby (1986), argue for a more historically contingent approach which emphasizes the variability, across time and space, of the social construction of the gendered division of labour. In her extensive review of the literature on gender and global capitalism, Redclift (1988: 433) concludes, 'the concrete manifestations of capitalism and patriarchy give rise to diverse outcomes which are the results of series of interactions between economic forms and between ideological representations and productive systems. . . . The articulation of capitalism with the sexual division of labour cannot be assumed to be uniform, but is a matter for concrete investigation'. This points to the need to treat abstractions as abstractions, not ossified laws for which history can only provide illustration. It is not a case of locating explanations for women's subordination exclusively at one level of analysis or another, but of retaining an awareness of the historical nature of totalities.

The second key debate, which is related to the problems of levels of analysis and the debates around theory versus history, is that of material versus ideological explanations. One of the major problems with feminism influenced by structuralist Marxism was the relegation of patriarchy to the ideological sphere, retaining the centrality of class at the economic level — the 'dual-systems' problem. This was the logical result of earlier interpretations of the mode of production as *material* production. The theoretical problem became how to connect patriarchal relations to capitalist production relations, rather than seeing them as part of capitalist production relations from the start. Armstrong and Armstrong (1983) argue for the inclusion of the sexual division of labour as integral to capitalist development – and thus refute both the term 'patriarchy' and 'dual-systems' theories – but they suggest we can accomplish this by 'stretching' already strained abstract principles of capitalist organization. I think that a more fundamental reconstruction of historical materialism is required if we are to understand, which I think we must, gender domination as irreducible to the logic of capital.

The sexual division of labour is crucial to understanding women's subordination, but reproduced patterns of gender domination, and the salience of gender in the construction of the differentiated subjects of capitalism, cannot be reduced to this. We need to see women not only in their relationship to an economic system, but also in relation to men and to each other. Thus, whether we call it 'patriarchy' or any analogous term,[5] we need a theory of gender to provide a way of organizing our insights into women's oppression. This does not imply, as structuralist Marxism tended to, that capitalist laws of motion provide the base with patriarchal ideologies filling in the superstructure. Rather, it recognizes that any historical social formation is a totality, in which the psychological, the economic, the personal and the political are inseparable. It is not a question of primacy between class and gender, or between production and consciousness, but an articulation of the material, ideological and psychodynamic base of each, their dynamics, and perhaps most importantly, how struggle on both ideological and material levels may be related. Feminist theory is vital to this project, and it is through analysis of this sort that it can best contribute to the development of socialist theory.

The third issue, and perhaps the most far-reaching in its consequences, is the question of 'difference'. Socialist feminists have had to deal seriously with charges of racism and Western bias in their construction of theories which are predicated on the relationship between class and gender hierarchies, to the outright neglect, or at best, the marginalization, of other axes of oppression. As Yuval-Davies and Anthias (1989: 8) suggest, 'the feminist literature on reproduction has generally failed to consider the reproduction of national, ethnic and racial categories'. This is related to the failure in Marxist-influenced theory more generally to theorize the subject in a non-essentialist manner. While I will examine in more detail the problem of exclusionary essentialism in feminist theory as it relates to the theorization of subjectivity in the next chapter, I want here to outline the broad challenge of anti-racist and post-colonial theorizing for developing socialist feminist theory.

Since the 1980s there has been a surge in publications which seek to integrate issues of race, ethnicity and nationality into feminist theory (Bhavnani and Coulson, 1986; hooks, 1990; Mohanty, 1991; Moraga and Anzaldúa, 1983; Ramazanoglu, 1989; Spelman, 1988; Spivak, 1987; Yuval-Davis and Anthias, 1989). As part of a broader literature associated with decolonization, they have questioned whether Western thought, including feminist thought, is able '. . .to encompass the critique of *Western* forms of domination' (Poster, 1989: 3 – emphasis added). Western-based, ahistorical notions of 'patriarchy' have, as Valverde (1985: 198) puts it, obscured the 'conflicts of interest between the women who pick coffee beans for fifty cents a day in Brazil and the white American feminist who sips coffee as she writes about women in general'. As I suggested in the previous chapter, many of the theoretical abstractions (for example, the separation of public and private and the association of women with domesticity) that have informed our theorizing have been based not only on a male perspective and periodization of history, but on one which is also white and Western. While socialist feminist theories are challenged to be more sensitive to differences between women, and to avoid unduly abstracting from the experience of white Western women to all women, the implications for theorizing go beyond this. bell hooks (1990: 21) provides a cogent critique of white feminists who, in response to efforts by women of colour to 'deconstruct' the category of women, 'responded by hearing only what was being said about race and racism'. This echoes the response of much malestream theory to the feminist critique. In both cases, the work of the marginalized 'Other' is 'relegated to the realm of the experiential'. As West (1988b: 18) argues, 'the time has passed when the so-called race question. . .can be relegated to secondary or tertiary theoretical significance' in either bourgeois or liberatory discourses. The decolonization movement extends feminism's critique of the gender divisions which have made Western modernity possible, to include other divisions on which Western 'progress' rests, and forces us to 'raise crucial questions regarding. . .the limited character of Marxist formulations of counterhegemonic projects against multi-leveled oppression'.

3.4   Towards Reconstruction

As Morrow (1991: 28) suggests, the challenge of the various crises in Marxism has opened new opportunities to develop a critical theory which incorporates 'structuralist, neo-Gramscian and post-structuralist methods and theoretical constructs without abandoning either an initial commitment to critical theory as a tradition of inquiry or its self-understanding as a political project and form of institutional analysis which has not altogether lost its roots in theories of social and cultural reproduction'. While in general agreement that this opportunity exists, I would add that the incorporation of the insights of feminist theory is crucial to this project.

Clearly, the Marxist paradigm of production, from which most theories of social reproduction have developed, needs to be transcended if multiple axes of oppression in the critique of capitalism can be adequately theorized. A number of emergent critical approaches which are influenced by — yet substantially reconstructive of — Marxism, may be instructive in this project. In general, they incorporate a shift in focus from the mode of production to processes of legitimation, the abandonment of an essentialist notion of structure, and a distinct attempt to overcome the dualism of subject and structure. Most visibly developed under the rubric of 'cultural studies', a transcendence of the earlier polarization of structuralism and culturalism, given impetus by the poststucturalist critique, is also evident in resistance theories in education and in some recent approaches to gender.

It was in the 'new' sociology of education that the debate between theories of social and cultural reproduction emerged most clearly in the 1970s. The attempt to overcome the impasses of that debate has resulted in the development of what have been termed 'resistance theories'. Reproduction theory in education has its roots in Althusser's identification of educational systems as ideological state apparatuses, and this was the grounding for the 'correspondence theory' of Bowles and Gintis (1976), which posited a structural relationship between the social organization of the school with the social organization of production. The education system, they argued, functions to prepare youth to take their places as workers, and thus is crucial in social reproduction. The culturalist moment in educational theory was represented primarily by Bourdieu (1977) and Bernstein (1977). Here the shift in focus was from social reproduction to cultural reproduction — less emphasis on the reproduction of the working class than on the reproduction of the dominant culture. There are sharp differences between these theories of social and cultural reproduction, but what often emerges is 'a one-sided emphasis on the systemic and deterministic aspects of social and cultural reproduction in capitalist societies. Not only are the voluntaristic aspects of struggle missing here, but also any hope of social change' (Giroux, 1981: 12). Resistance theories grew out of these inadequacies of theories of social and cultural reproduction, are more concerned with education as a basis for transformation and exhibit a more crucial distance from seeing class domination as the only mode of oppression in capitalist societies. As Morrow and Torres (1987: 40) characterize this turn in educational research, it represents a move toward 'more open models of social and cultural reproduction which attempt to examine manifestations of resistance, draw out the significance of the cultural dimensions of reproduction, provide the basis for an understanding of the subjects of the educational process and their relationship to the curriculum, and attempt to restore the dialectic between correspondence and contradiction'. O'Brien (1984) has suggested that the development of 'hegemonic analysis' within educational theory could be useful for feminist theory. Its appropriation of certain key themes in critical theory warrants closer attention.

A different tack in the critique of earlier conceptions of social and cultural reproduction has been taken by some works specifically concerned with gender. Representative here are the Australian theorists Clare Burton and R.W. Connell. Burton (1985) is critical of the functionalist implications of much social reproduction theory as it has been applied to the study of women's subordination, but she remains committed to the utility of the concept of social reproduction itself. Her concern is with the 'changing but enduring' nature of sexual inequalities: 'I am concerned with the ways in which these are reproduced, because unless we understand the basis of their durability in rapidly changing circumstances, effective political interventions to eliminate them will be neither adequately formulated nor acted upon' (Burton, 1985: xii). Her strategy is to develop a framework for 'an extended theory of social reproduction', which sees gender and class as 'so inextricably linked that neither assumes a primary or determining place', and which refocuses attention from the mode of production to processes of legitimation in capitalist social formations. In doing so, she brings together a number of important insights from various strands of feminist thought, taking into account the state, educational systems, biological reproduction, the institution of the family and the labour process, but in the end falls back on 'social reproduction' as an explanatory concept. Yet, as Giddens (1981: 64) stresses, social reproduction is not an explanatory concept in itself, but rather something which requires explanation.

Connell takes a strong position against 'the' theory of social reproduction (grouping Althusser, Lefebvre and Bourdieu together), suggesting that it is inherently functionalist and holds little liberatory potential. In adopting the concept of social reproduction, he charges Marxist-feminist reproduction theory with tying itself 'in extraordinary knots, trying to extract explanatory principles from Lacan, Levi-Strauss, semiotics. . .with. . .a complete lack of success' (Connell, 1983: 55). He charges that: '[T]he concept of "social reproduction". . .makes sense only if an invariant structure is postulated at the start. History enters the theory as something *added on* to the basic cycle of structural reproduction' (Connell, 1987: 44).

Connell's critique is valid only if we accept his tarring of any theory which speaks of social and cultural reproduction with the same functionalist, structuralist brush. His insistence that we see social structure as being constantly *constituted* as opposed to being constantly *reproduced* is convincing, but only if we retain the notion from theories of reproduction that patriarchal-capitalist social structures have historically been constituted in rather a consistent manner, without *total* contingency. It would otherwise make little sense to speak, as Connell himself does, of 'a historically composed gender order' (1987: 159).

Despite my reservations about his abandonment of the concept of social reproduction altogether, I concur with many of Connell's criticisms of earlier approaches, and accept many of the arguments he advances for the development of a more adequate theory. In particular, attention needs to be paid to two of his arguments. First, it is essential to see that 'Gender is *part* of the "relations of production", and has been from the start; it is not just mixed up in their reproduction' (Connell, 1987: 45). Second, social reproduction needs to be viewed as 'an object of strategy': 'Groups that hold power do try to reproduce the structure that gives them their privilege. But it is always an open question whether, and how, they will succeed' (Connell, 1987: 44).

What conclusions, then, can we draw about the concept of social reproduction? Connell (1987) suggests that any theory of social reproduction must answer two questions: 'What is being reproduced?', and 'How is the reproducing accomplished?'. Is social reproduction, as Connell (1987: 44) suggests, a concept which makes sense only 'if an invariant structure is postulated at the start'? Connell's critique rests on the assumption that 'social' equals 'structure' and this is what is being reproduced. With this interpretation, it is a valid critique, and the concept of social reproduction should rightly be abandoned. If, however, we conceive of 'social' not as structural, but as relational, there are grounds for retaining the notion of social reproduction as an important concept for feminist analysis. Connell is correct in asserting that 'social structure must be seen as constantly constituted rather than constantly reproduced' (p. 44), but a feminist analysis sees structure as being constantly constituted in a way which reproduces a fundamental relational asymmetry between women and men — actually, between women and fully individuated, autonomous human beings as they have been theoretically and practically constructed. It is this asymmetry, not any particular 'invariant' structure, which is being reproduced. It is first and foremost not a question of absolute difference but one of how difference is imbued with meaning and constructed as hierarchy.

The problematic status of social reproduction as a theoretical concept is related to some of the fundamental problems in existing formulations of the critique of capitalist patriarchy that I reviewed in the last chapter: the conflation of the gender division of labour with the public–private division, the lack of an adequate dialectic between processes of accumulation and processes of legitimation, and an underemphasis on possibilities for transformation, rather than reproduction, of the existing gender order. Following from Marx's famous dictum that the point is not just to describe the world, a critical theory must also ask the question of how we can encourage transformation rather than reproduction of an oppressive order. As Aronowitz and Giroux (1985: 73) suggest, to do so requires that we 'reconstruct the major theories of reproduction in order to abstract from them their most radical and emancipatory insights'.

A renewed emphasis on human agency refocuses the analysis to the way in which human actors seek to come to terms with immediate circumstances and problems, the way in which structures circumscribe their possibilities for action, and how in turn, they are reproduced by that action. Reproduction becomes an outcome of strategies situated in a web of power relationships; thus 'if reproduction predominates in a given case, it is because that side of things has won out in a contest with other tendencies, not because it is guaranteed by some sociological law' (Connell et al., 1982: 190). As outlined above, central to both structural and psychoanalytic theories of social reproduction is explication of why things *don't* change. As Aronowitz and Giroux (1985: 70) put it, they lack 'a language of possibility'. Lines of inquiry must be opened around the relationship of subject and structure, culture and ideology, and 'myth' and 'fact' in the constitution of social reality, and the construction and regulation of individual and collective identities, with an eye to identifying 'fault lines' in the social order. Only then can we begin to consider the possibility of transformation.

In this chapter I have traced the shifts and turns in the 'reproduction problematic' as socialist and feminist theories began to pose questions which the traditional Marxist concern with the capital–wage labour relationship had marginalized. The systematicity of the orthodox Marxist conception of social reproduction was fundamentally challenged, both from within a fragmented 'Western Marxism' and from emerging poststructuralist critiques. Feminist scholarship has demanded that the problematic of social reproduction is fundamentally one about the subject–structure relationship, and has insisted 'against marxism's claims that the determining social relationship is between wage labour and capital, exploiter and exploited, proletarian and capitalist', that 'subjective identity is also constructed as masculine or feminine, placing the individual as husband or wife, mother or father, son or daughter' (Alexander, 1984: 132).

In the critique of socialist theory, feminists have concentrated on trying to demonstrate the integral role of sexual oppression to the capitalist structure. As Rabine (1988: 25) suggests, however, a more fruitful strategy may be to take what critics such as Perry Anderson (1983) decry as the 'supplementarity' of feminism — its *lack* of a centralization of the structures of women's oppression — as its strength. In other words, we need to move beyond the feminist critique of socialist theory to 'the imagining of a liberatory radical theory of socialism that would more adequately address interlocking systems of domination like sexism, racism, class oppression, imperialism, and so on' (hooks, 1991: 28). The chapters to follow will suggest how feminist theory might begin to reconstruct a critical theoretical project which embraces these insights, beginning with the theorization of subjectivity.

4

Gendered Identities

In this chapter I intend to examine some of the debates around 'the subject' — specifically the subject of feminist theory but also more generally the subject of *social* theory. The word 'subject', of course, has a dual meaning — as the signifier of the individual who has a subjectivity, and as the signifier of one who is under the authority of another. While poststructuralist theories stress the coincidence of these meanings, epitomized in the assertion by Foucault (1980: 97) that 'we should try to grasp subjection in its material instance as a constitution of subjects', theories of social and cultural reproduction, including most socialist feminist theories, emphasize the subject as the location of (potentially resistive) agency. The notion of 'gendered subjectivity', in both these senses, has garnered considerable interest in feminist theory, and is central to an understanding of the way in which gender becomes embedded in both subject and structure, and their relationship. Whether through psychoanalytic exploration of the roots of gender identity, or through the continuous process of gender socialization which reproduces 'femininity' and 'masculinity', the overriding question has been why 'women seem to "internalize" the oppressive "external" reality' (Jaggar, 1983: 149) and thus collude in its reproduction. As Jaggar suggests, socialist feminist theory needs to develop an alternative to the traditional Marxist notion of 'false consciousness', the concept of 'sex-role conditioning' implied in liberal feminist thought, and the implicit pessimism of some psychoanalytic approaches. Social reproduction involves a legitimizing process; yet rather than seeing the dominant ideology as being uncritically 'transmitted' to reproduce the conditions for class and gender inequalities, it is more fruitful to examine the negotiation of social ideology in the context of lived experience. This differs from the phenomenological and ethnomethodological approaches which stress the negotiation of intersubjective situations (without reference to structures of power), yet borrows from this tradition in seeing gender identity as something which is 'accomplished' through practice. That is, it recognizes agency on the part of the subject.

4.1   Beyond the Production Paradigm

Any theory of social reproduction must include explanation at the level of the subject — thus accepting the Weberian insight that 'structures', no matter how compelling, 'act' only through individual subjectivities. I want to begin, as Dorothy Smith (1987: 99) suggests a feminist sociology must, with the problematic formulated by Marx and Engels (1845–6/1970): 'Individuals always started, and always start, from themselves. Their relations are the relations of their real life. How does it happen that their relations assume an independent existence over against them? And that the forces of their own life overpower them?'

Related to this is another central problematic, also clearly outlined by Marx in the *Economic and Philosophical Manuscripts* (1844, in Bottomore, 1963: 158):

> Though each person is a unique individual — and it is just that particularity which makes each an individual, a really individual communal being — each is equally the whole, the ideal whole, the subjective existence of society as thought and experienced. Each exists in reality as the representation and the real mind of social existence, and as the sum of human manifestations of life.

In this passage, Marx sets out the subject–structure relationship as simultaneously individual and social. In some ways, he anticipates the later work of symbolic interactionism (such as that of Mead), which stresses the self as constituted through the internalization of the social; but unlike the latter, domination is central to Marx. The elements of a critical social psychology and a theory of the subject are set out, but there is a key theoretical space in reconciling the actor, as the bearer of socially imposed identities, as both an individual and a collective subject. While Marx admirably outlines the terrain, he fails to explore it fully.

Of the challenges levelled against marxism, both from feminist and non-feminist writers, perhaps the most serious is that regarding the theorization of the 'subject'. MacDonald (1991) suggests that it is in their questioning of the 'subject' that Marxists, feminists and poststructuralists have found some intellectual affinity. Specifically, there is increasing doubt cast on the premise of orthodox Marxist theory that an individual's identity, consciousness, and in essence, social being, are derived from one's position in the social division of labour. 'Subjects' in orthodox Marxism are positioned as bourgeois or proletariat, owner or worker — as members of a class. The concept of class thus problematizes the relationship between individuals as they appear as workers and owners, and between the individual and society. Feminist deployment of the concept of gender has recast that relationship to problematize both the relationship between men and women, and between women and society. This insistence, that subjects are not only classed, but also gendered, has taken socialist feminist theory into a multitude of directions seeking to unravel the knots of just how gender constitutes the subject. Yet most of this work has remained within the parameters of the 'paradigm of production'.

A focus on 'production', even if broadly taken to include both the 'production of things' and the 'production of life', is inadequate for the development of feminist ontology. One of the obvious problems with approaches that seek to insert biological reproduction and reproductive labour into a production model is that gender comes to be understood solely in reproductive terms. One might be forgiven, when reading most of these accounts, for thinking that human reproduction has little to do with feelings such as intimacy, pleasure, guilt, passion, or for that matter, anything to do with sexuality at all.[1] To begin to theorize the subject adequately, we need to return to Marx's starting point of 'sensuous human activity' as the basis of subjectivity, and then radically reconstruct his project to remove the limits placed on it by the production paradigm. This entails moving towards a paradigm of intersubjectivity, built on the relationship of subject to subject, not subject to object.

Perhaps the most radical recasting of historical materialism has been Habermas's displacement of production as the basic human activity for an emphasis on communicative action. 'The production paradigm so restricts the concept of practice that the question arises of how the paradigmatic activity-type of labour or the making of products is related to all the other cultural forms of expression of subjects capable of speech and action' (Habermas, 1985/1987b: 79). Recent feminist philosophy has offered a particularly pointed challenge to the production paradigm, asking whether 'the concept of production, which is based on the model of an active subject transforming, making and shaping an object given to it' can adequately comprehend traditionally female activities, such as child-rearing and care-giving, 'which are so thoroughly intersubjective' (Benhabib and Cornell, 1987: 2).

One of the consequences of adherence to the production model as paradigmatic of human activity is the emphasis on external forms of domination. For Marx, productive relations take on a mystified form, allowing capital to present itself as objective and present its power as derived from natural relations rather than social relations of domination. As Sherover-Marcuse (1986: 126) suggests, Marx failed to theorize the *materiality* of mystified consciousness, that is, he failed to recognize that 'mystified consciousness is not merely a set of false ideas or illusions but that it encompasses modes of being, ways of acting and of experiencing oneself and one's existence to which people have become accustomed, attached and even "addicted" on an affective level'. It is the materiality of experienced forms of mystified consciousness that 'congeals into "character structures" and "personality types" ', what Sherover-Marcuse calls 'naturalized and normalized cages for the individuals who inhabit them'. By focusing on the reproduction of domination at the level of the system, Marxism failed to comprehend the significance of the reproduction of domination at the level of individual subjectivities.

Feminist theory and practice have long recognized the subjective dimension of the reproduction of domination — it was this recognition that made 'consciousness-raising' an essential part of feminist struggle. Yet a feminist theory of subjectivity must not be construed merely in terms of the opposition of femininity and individuality, and a fundamentally different approach must be undertaken.

4.2   The Autonomous Ego?

4.2.1   The early Frankfurt School

It was the lack of a theory of subjectivity that led to attempts at a synthesis of Freud and Marx, most notably by key figures associated with the Frankfurt School. Inspired by the earlier Hegelian Marxism of Lukács and Korsch, members of the Frankfurt School turned increasingly away from production to the analysis of culture and ideology in an attempt to theorize the eclipse of class consciousness. Central here was the insistence on a psychological component to the Marxian theory of false consciousness — 'that the equation of false consciousness with ideologies must be supplemented by a psychological analysis of the motivations behind their acceptance' (Jay, 1984: 204). Thus came the first systematic integration of Freudian psychoanalysis into Marxist theory, initially undertaken by Erich Fromm. The focal point for this integration of Freud and Marx in critical theory was to be elaborated in their analysis of the family. The family was the site of the development of subjectivity, the meeting point of individual and society. The central interest here was in uncovering the social creation of psychological structures conducive to domination. As Fromm put it, 'the family is the medium through which the society or the social class stamps its specific structure on the child, and hence on the adult. The family is the psychological agency of society' (1932/ 1978: 483).

In Horkheimer's 'Authority and the Family', the family occupies a contradictory space in capitalist society — on the one hand, it 'educates for authority in bourgeois society', yet on the other it 'cultivates the dream of a better condition for mankind' (Horkheimer, 1972: 114). While enmeshed in market relationships, the family nonetheless offers an emancipatory potential. According to such writers as Lasch (1979), the family is portrayed here as a refuge from the public world where individuals can escape from instrumentality, where they can be treated as human beings, not objects. Yet Horkheimer also realizes the price this extracts from women: 'the present-day family is a source of strength to resist the total dehumanization of the world and contains an element of antiauthoritarianism. But it must also be recognized that because of her dependence woman herself has been changed. . . .[H]er own development is lastingly restricted' (1972: 118). The emancipatory potential, then, is only for males, and rests in the maintenance of patriarchal authority in the family. Following a Freudian theory of socialization, Horkheimer posits that the internalization of paternal authority by sons is the internalization of both bourgeois authority and the autonomy to resist authority. Unfortunately, this autonomy is not available to women, and as paternal authority wanes under the increasingly administered society, it becomes less available to males. Thus, Horkheimer and Adorno are later forced to lament the decline of patriarchy as leading to the decline of the autonomous individual, and thus the decline of any possibility of emancipatory subjectivities. In their hands, the 'decline of subjectivity' became central – the notion that human beings had become so totally dominated that there was no possibility of emancipatory struggle. Theory became ideology critique, with little relation to praxis. As Agger (1977: 16) notes, 'both economism and critical theory withdrew from the imperative of revolutionary practice, the one thinking that the revolution would occur without subjectivity (or, strictly speaking, that the correct subjectivity would arise automatically in response to economic suffering), the other thinking that subjectivity did not exist'.

4.2.2 Habermas

I referred, in chapter 1, to Habermas's 'reconstruction' of historical materialism based on the distinction between labour and interaction, and between system interaction and social interaction. Within this model, Habermas also seeks to insert a cognitive and moral dimension which he claims overcomes the philosophy of the subject which has plagued Marxism. Essentially, what he is positing is an evolutionary model of social change in which not only structure is transformed, but the subject, and the subject–structure relationship. That is, a transformation in social formation requires a transformation in individual identity and character.

Habermas explicitly rejects both the pessimism and the uni-dimensional conception of rationalization embodied in the work of the earlier Frankfurt theorists. As Morrow (1988: 3) summarizes it, 'whereas the early studies were concerned primarily with the social psychology of domination', Habermas is also concerned with 'an orientation toward grounding normative claims and a constructive theory of emancipation'. Where for Horkheimer and Adorno, the spread of instrumental rationality increasingly subordinates all levels of existence – production, culture, personality – to its logic of calculation, Habermas introduces a more complex model of social development. Drawing on the developmental models of Piaget and Kohlberg, Habermas incorporates a cognitive dimension into his model of societal evolution. The theory of communicative action is based on the evolutionary differentiation of system and lifeworld, guided by distinctly different types of rationalizing processes. He thus denies the implied 'functional fit' between the economy, culture and personality (Benhabib, 1986: 230). Through this strategy, he claims to have overcome the philosophy of the subject which assumed a 'transcendental consciousness', by focusing on 'concrete forms of life':

> In culturally embodied self-understandings, intuitively present group solidarities, and the competencies of socialized individuals that are brought into play as know-how, the reason expressed in communicative action is mediated with the traditions, social practices, and body-centred complexes of experience that coalesce into *particular* totalities (Habermas, 1987b: 326).

It is with this conception of the subject that he revives the 'autonomous ego' abandoned by Adorno and Horkheimer. Yet he retains an androcentric view of the subject – a view premised upon the abstract individual, which, since the very 'discovery' of the individual in social philosophy, has been inherently male. As he understands it, moral self-development parallels the development of normative structures, from concrete and particular to abstract and general. The end result is, as Leonard (1990: 46) concludes, that

Habermas 'is unable to break from the "universalistic" assumptions that have plagued attempts to realize "critical reason" since, perhaps, the Enlightenment itself'.

4.2.3   *The feminist critique of the autonomous ego*

From Hegel, through Marx and the early Frankfurt School, to work by Habermas, some notion of the 'autonomous ego' — the fully individuated and somehow disembodied subject — has been the presupposition of any theory of resistance. Yet as Stephanie Engel (1980: 103) notes, this ideal, 'is not in any *a priori* sense a moral or human given'. Most significantly, feminist theorists 'have begun to articulate conceptions of autonomy that are premised not simply on separation but also on the experiences of mutuality, relatedness and the recognition of an other as a full subject'. This entails not a rejection of the concept of autonomy, but a critical reinterpretation.

I want to focus here on some of the feminist work which has radically questioned the conceptions of autonomy and individuality in these 'critical' social psychologies. Of particular interest here are Jessica Benjamin's work on Adorno and Horkheimer, Carol Gilligan's on Kohlberg and Seyla Benhabib's on Habermas.

For Benjamin, what is lacking in the social psychology of Adorno and Horkheimer is a concept of intersubjectivity — 'of subject to subject relations': 'The world is not conceived of as an intersubjective realm in which the objects encountered are really themselves subjects who have the capacity to act and be affected by another's actions' (1977: 49). Lacking this concept, they are forced into an uncritical acceptance of a Freudian conception of the ego, tied to the internalization of authority, inherently resulting in the view that 'authority is in some sense seen as necessary or even vindicated' (Benjamin, 1977: 42). The product is an individual psychology rather than a social, intersubjective psychology, which undermines the critical project of emancipation. The consequences for women are most clearly drawn out in their analysis of the family. Through their reliance on a Freudian internalization of paternal authority as the basis of the later rejection of authority on the part of autonomous (male) individuals, they collapse individuality into masculinity. Benjamin offers a reinterpretation of emancipatory potential based not upon identification with the paternal authority figure, but 'based on identification with others stemming from awareness of one's own suffering and oppression. The knowledge which is based upon paying attention to one's feelings and denied aspirations implies, ultimately, a different view of human nature and civilizing process as well' (1978: 56). While Benjamin's work is important in exposing the masculinity of critical theory's conception of the subject through her emphasis on intersubjectivity, it is problematic in its implicit valorization of the feminine.

Gilligan's research on Kohlberg's developmental psychology remains a key work in the feminist critique of the 'autonomous ego'. Kohlberg posits six stages of moral development, the sixth and highest stage representing universalistic reasoning. It rests on a conception of justice rooted in a 'rights conception of morality' which 'is geared to arriving at an objectively fair or just resolution to moral dilemmas upon which all rational persons could agree' (Gilligan, 1982: 19–20). Women appear to be stuck in a lower level of development, in a conception of morality based on caring and on responsibility for others. Gilligan argues that Kohlberg's masculine bias fails to consider the greater emphasis that women place on context and the concrete effects of their decisions on other people. As she summarizes it:

> The elusive mystery of women's development lies in its recognition of the continuing importance of attachment in the human life cycle. Woman's place in man's life cycle is to protect this recognition while the developmental litany intones the celebration of separation, autonomy, individuation and natural rights (p. 23).

While Gilligan's work has been rightly criticized for making generalizations about gendered ethics based on a sample of white, middle-class, American girls, and for a tendency to over-romanticize women's moral decision-making processes, what is important about her work is the questions it raises about a universalistic ethic based on principles of abstract, versus concrete, individualism.

Gilligan's insights have been usefully developed by Seyla Benhabib (1986, 1987) in her work on Habermas's developmental subject. For Benhabib, Habermas ultimately fails by restricting the ideal of autonomy to the standpoint of the 'generalized other':

This results in a corresponding inability to treat human needs, desires, and emotions in any other way than by abstracting away from them and by condemning them to silence. . . .Institutional justice is thus seen as representing a higher stage of moral development than interpersonal responsibility, care, love, and solidarity; the respect for rights and duties is regarded as prior to care and concern about another's need; moral cognition precedes moral affect; the mind, we may summarize, is the sovereign of the body, and reason, the judge of inner nature (1986: 342).

Benhabib suggests, in contrast, that the perspectives of the 'generalized other' and the 'concrete other' must be treated as complementary, that the 'ideal community of communication corresponds to an ego identity which allows the unfolding of the relation to the *concrete other* on the basis of *autonomous action*' (p. 342). Thus, while endorsing the paradigm shift from production to communication, she seeks to re-orient Habermas's disembodied, autonomous ego to recognition of the concrete and particular.

What is important to all these critiques is the emphasis on intersubjectivity, recognition of the particularity of others, and rejection of the privileging of reason over affectivity which is implied in androcentric models of individuated, autonomous subjectivity. The familiar Cartesian dualism of mind and body underlies the 'disembedding' of the reasoning, mature, capable-of-resistance social actor. Habermas notes that 'reason. . .has no body, cannot suffer, and also arouses no passion' (Habermas, 1982: 221) and he himself clings to such a concept of the reasoning subject. It seems appropriate then to begin by conceptualizing the subject as an *embodied* subject. Bodies, of course, are necessary to any conception of human beings as agents, actors or individuals. A body is necessary to the concept of labour — it is with the body that one presents oneself as a labourer and performs work. A body is especially important when we wish to speak about subjects as 'men' or 'women', as it is the most obvious signifier of those categories. It is only through recognition of embodiment that we can recognize particularity. Yet almost without exception, theories of the subject, and of subjectivity, treat self-awareness and consciousness as somehow dependent on transcending bodily existence, rather than as coming to terms with it. It is on this point that feminist theories of the subject have both flourished and floundered — flourished in their exposing of the androcentric bias of grand theories of 'unencumbered selves' and floundered in implicitly or explicitly replicating gender polarity,[2] or the binary opposition of male and female, rooted in bodily existence. In feminist theories of the subject, it has become an opposition between 'essentialism' and 'nominalism' (Alcoff, 1988).

4.3   Feminist Theories of the Subject: Essentialism versus Nominalism

4.3.1   *Feminist essentialism: biology, philosophy and history*

The tendency towards essentialism in socialist feminist theory is linked to the underlying humanism of Marxist social theory in general – the assumption of 'common essential features in terms of which human beings can be defined and understood' (Soper, 1986: 12). It is this core of humanity that makes sense of such conceptual terms as alienation, consciousness and agency.

Feminist essentialism is by no means a unitary stream of thought. Three types of essentialist thinking can be identified, each resting on different sorts of argument about how biological difference is transformed into subjective difference – biological essentialism, philosophical essentialism, and historical reification. The specificity of the female body, and in particular its connection to the reproduction of the species, is implicated in each argument. Thus, each form of essentialism is, in a sense, biological, but the nature of the arguments developed differ considerably.

Biological essentialism, while usually roundly denounced, characterizes a range of feminist theory. Examples here are the books by Shulamith Firestone (1970), Mary Daly (1978) and Adrienne Rich (1977). Firestone attempted to build a materialist analysis, not of economic class, but of 'sex class'. The basis of her account is that 'unlike economic class, sex class sprang directly from a biological reality: men and women were created different, and not equally privileged' (1970: 8). Women, she suggests, are 'at the continual mercy of their biology', which makes them dependent on males for survival. She conflates biology with procreation, and outlines a feminist strategy as the development and control of technology which will liberate women from their biological enslavement. Thus, Firestone deplores biology as the basis, not of women's identity in any constructive sense but of an identity which grounds their oppression.

Daly (1978) evaluates female biology more positively, and theorizes a biological essentialism which privileges women. Women are life-giving and hence life-affirming – men are barren and thus must prey on female energy. Men are 'parasitic', they 'passionately identify' with the foetus, they aspire to be 'supermothers controlling biological mothers':

> The male "mother's" spiritual "fecundity" depends upon his fetal (fatal) fettering of the female to whom he eternally attaches himself by a male-made umbilical cord, extracting nutrients and excreting waste (as he does also with "Mother Earth"). The penis, of course, is both a material and symbolic instrument for the restoration and maintenance of this umbilical attachment (Daly, 1978: 60–1).

Daly clearly finds the male/female analog in culture/nature, positing a continuity between femaleness and nature in which lies true humanity. Men are thus a threat to women/nature, inescapably due to their biological inability to give and affirm life.

Rich (1977: 21) also posits a direct relationship between women's biology and their consciousness:

> [F]emale biology – the diffuse, intense sensuality radiating out from clitoris, breasts, uterus, vagina; the lunar cycles of menstruation; the gestation and fruition of life which can take place in the female body – has far more radical implications than we have yet come to appreciate. . . .We must touch the unity and resonance of our physicality, our bond with the natural order, the corporeal ground of our intelligence.

Both Daly and Rich encourage feminism to embrace women's biological specificity as the grounding of a woman-centred valorization of 'femaleness'. It is our biology which gives us our essence.

Philosophical essentialism is best represented by Simone de Beauvoir and Mary O'Brien, both of whom have provided tremendously influential theories of gender-differentiated subjectivity in which women's sense of self is located in the particularity of the female body, but a particularity in the metaphysical sense.

Simone de Beauvoir (1949/1961: 249) writes that 'One is not born but becomes a woman'. This fundamental precept is the girder of feminist social theory. It would seem to belie a biological essentialism, but the manner in which de Beauvoir develops it stands firmly on a philosophical essentialism, rooted in women's bodily existence.[3] In the introductory section on 'destiny', de Beauvoir rejects the respective 'monisms' of biological determinism, psychoanalysis (Freud) and historical materialism (Engels). Her strategy is to incorporate certain insights of each of these into a more culturally sensitive framework, asserting that 'The value of muscular strength, of the phallus, of the tool can be defined only in a world of values; it is determined by the basic project through which the existent seeks transcendence' (p. 55). The rest of the book is primarily an exploration of the means by which culture 'cuts off' the feminine body from the possibility of transcendence. Central to the denial of transcendence to women is their 'enslavement to the generative function' (p. 108). This enslavement is the basis for her invocation of the universality of women as 'Other', a category 'as primordial as consciousness itself' (p. xvi). By clinging to a Hegelian notion of transcendence as transcendence of the body, she posits that as long as women are bound by their reproductive capacities, they will remain the eternal 'Other', unable to attain full autonomy. It is a reproductive entrapment of consciousness.

O'Brien's critique of de Beauvoir centres on the latter's entirely negative interpretation of the reproductive experience: 'She sees human reproduction as indistinguishable from that of other animal species, making reproductive labour a labour immune to the interpretations of a rational consciousness and incapable of forming an authentically human consciousness' (O'Brien, 1981: 75). O'Brien posits a reproductive consciousness, again rooted in bodily existence, which provides a privileged continuity to women which is denied to men. Men are *forced* to transcend their bodily existence, in a vain and artificial attempt to capture reproductive continuity. Thus, against de Beauvoir, who analysed human reproduction as essentially alienating for women, O'Brien finds it alienating for men. The reproductive process thus creates two gender-specific types of consciousness. The implications of this analysis include a twist on Freud's dictum of anatomy as destiny: 'Men are necessarily rooted in biology, and their physiology is their fate' (O'Brien, 1981: 192).

Thus, both de Beauvoir and O'Brien, while differently evaluating the biological experience of reproduction for women's subjectivity, locate an essential gendered subjectivity in the bodily parameters of reproduction. Both invoke a universal principle of consciousness which, interpreted in terms of reproductive imperatives, privileges one sex over the other, and creates a gender-differentiated subjectivity.

Most socialist feminist theory tends toward essentialism based on a historical reification of women's experience and a corresponding reification of 'gender identity'. Taking their cue from Marx, they locate subjectivity and consciousness not in a biological or philosophical essence, but in human activity, primarily as it is organized under capitalism. Gender identity is rooted in the sexual division of labour. One of the first, and most influential statements of this stream of thought was developed by Rosaldo (1974),[4] who posited that women's lower status was the result of a universal division of human activity into 'public' and 'private' spheres, with women confined to the latter. The private sphere was that which was organized around mothers and their children − work in this sphere, done by women, was always valued less than work done in the public sphere by men. Chodorow (1978), Dinnerstein (1976) and Ortner (1974) all draw on this public−private split, and women's role in mothering within the private sphere, as crucial in the development of gender identity. The historical reification and conflation of public/private, production/reproduction, male/female also characterizes the bulk of Marxist feminist theory which focused on the gendered division of labour in capitalism as rooted in the exigencies of biological reproduction. For example, Armstrong and Armstrong (1983: 9) base their argument on the fact that 'women, not men, have babies':

[F]ree wage labour, which is essential to the very definition of capitalism, entails the reproduction of labour power primarily at another location. This separation under capitalism between commodity production and human reproduction (including the reproduction of the commodity labour power) in turn implies a particular division of labour between the sexes, and thus a division within classes. It is a division that. . .is fundamental to the understanding of how the capitalist production system operates at all levels of abstraction and of how and under what conditions people will rebel.

This is the material basis of 'the' ideology of gender, and the construction of femininity and masculinity (Armstrong and Armstrong, 1984).

Several important challenges to essentialist formulations of women's nature can be identified. The first challenge came from the dissenting voices of women of colour, lesbians, working-class women and third-world women. As they entered feminist discourse, they found little resonance in their own lives in the archetype of the dependent, heterosexual, Western, full-time mother upon which the historical reification of 'gender identity' was constructed. Feminist theory replicated the construction of a bourgeois subject (as did the earlier attempts at Freudo-Marxian synthesis) based on the experience of the white, bourgeois two-parent household. The challenge from historical investigation of the meaning of 'gender' also illustrates that it is a far from stable conceptual category (Riley, 1988). Marx (1973: 105) might be heeded in his assertion that:

[E]ven the most abstract categories, despite their validity – precisely because of their abstractness – for all epochs are nevertheless, in the specific character of this abstraction, themselves likewise a product of historical relations, and possess their full validity only for and within those relations.

Another important challenge is linked with the more general critique of humanism embodied in the proliferation of poststructuralist theories.

4.3.2   Deconstructing 'woman': poststructuralist feminism

Poststructuralist theories reject the concept of the humanist subject, whose essential core is repressed by society and who lies in wait of our peeling back of culture to find it. Poststructuralist feminism approaches the subject and subjectivity in a way that poses a radical challenge to essentialism. The focus of analysis is shifted from the subject as a manifestation of her/his 'essence' to the 'subject in process' — never unitary, never complete. Rather than looking to universals such as reproductive capacities, our gaze is directed to the realm of the symbolic — most significantly, to language — as implicated most centrally in the construction of 'men' and 'women'. This is captured in Kristeva's conception of the 'speaking subject'. Language is not an expression of some pre-existing subjectivity — instead, 'an individual's subjectivity is constituted in language for her every time she speaks' (Weedon, 1987: 88). 'Femininity', for Kristeva, is not a property of the subject, but of language. As such, its meaning can never be fixed. She asks, 'What can "identity", even "sexual identity" mean in a new theoretical and scientific space where the very notion of identity is challenged?' (Kristeva, 1982: 51–2). Because Kristeva sees 'woman' as something that 'cannot be represented', 'a feminist practice can be only negative. . .so that we may say "that's not it" and "that's still not it" ' (Kristeva, 1981: 137). This radically anti-essentialist stance culminates, as Fraser (1992a: 66) suggests, in a *post*-feminist stance, where collective identities such as 'feminist' may actually be perceived as totalitarian and dangerous.

Another poststructuralist tack is suggested by Foucault's conception of power as plural and not entirely negative, and his deconstructive approach to the 'subject'. For Foucault, the subject is decentred and dispersed, constituted in a multiplicity of power relations that produce meanings. Foucault demands that we forswear 'totalizing' discourses and reject the model of the rational humanist subject as an accomplice to disciplinary power.

An influential feminist account, inspired by Foucault, is that of Judith Butler, who appropriates Foucault's method of 'genealogy' to deconstruct the 'subject' of feminism. Butler contests the 'reification' of gender implicit in binary conceptions of masculine/feminine subjectivity, suggesting that any notion of 'feminine identity' as the foundation for feminist politics is mistaken. Such a foundation can only be constraining, as it obscures the 'field of power' through which the subject is formed (1990: 6). For Butler (1990: 33), 'Gender is the repeated stylization of the body, a set of repeated acts within a highly rigid regulatory frame that congeal over time to produce the appearance of substance, of a natural sort of being.'

Gender is thus *performative*, 'it has no ontological status apart from the various acts which constitute its reality' (p. 136). Gender is an *effect* of performance — it is constituted in the performance. Her feminist strategy, then, is to disrupt the performance, to 'trouble' the congealed categories of gender through parody. Butler's work is important in its insistence that there is no 'essence' reflected by gender — it only takes on a guise of naturalness through repeated, and discursively constructed, performance.

The appeal of poststructuralist accounts which dismantle the legitimacy of the categories which constrain us is evident. As hooks (1990: 29) suggests, 'critiques of essentialism which challenge notions of universality and static over-determined identity within mass culture and mass consciousness can open up new possibilities for the construction of self and the assertion of agency'. While feminist—poststructuralist alliances have pointed to these possibilities, there are several key problems with a wholesale adoption of a poststructuralist stance on the subject. First, while we may rightly criticize Marxism for its faith in pre-given objective 'interests' from which subjectivity will automatically spring, it is equally untenable to suggest that nothing exists outside its construction in discourse. As Hawkesworth (1989: 55) points out, women's accounts of rape, domestic violence or sexual harassment (to name just a few material realities) 'are not fictions or figurations that admit of the free play of signification'.

Secondly, poststructuralist critiques of the feminist subject are often predicated on the inability of more 'essentialist' formulations to take into account differences between women, such as those of sexual orientation, class and race, yet they rarely include any substantial discussion of the materiality of these differences 'once they have served their theoretical purpose of dissuading feminists from claiming commonalities across class and racial lines' (Modleski, 1991: 18). This is to deny the crucial role that subjugated groups have played in rethinking the whole notion of identity. As Waugh (1989: 3) suggests, 'for those marginalized by the dominant culture, a sense of identity as constructed through impersonal and social relations of power (rather than a sense of identity as the reflection of an inner "essence") has been a major aspect of their self-concept long before poststructuralists and postmodernists began to assemble their cultural manifestos'. The neglect of this insight leads to the problem of articulating notions of collective identity or struggle within the parameters of poststructuralism, and seems less than helpful in assisting feminism in its attempts to recover subjectivity and agency – in essence, a history – for marginalized groups. '[The] recurrent motif of the "death of the subject" in poststructuralist and postmodern thought raises the question ". . .which subject"?: eliding subjectivity with the abstract individualism of patriarchal bourgeois humanism, such a claim ignores the new emerging discourses of subjectivity and their link to emancipatory struggles' (Felski, 1989b: 230).

Finally, the refusal of a 'subject' for feminist theory leads to serious problems with the status of poststructuralist feminism as a political project. Not only does it have difficulty in accounting for its own emergence as a non-repressive discourse, but its inherent relativism poses clear difficulties for the inherently normative character of feminism. As Nancy Fraser (1989: 29) asks of Foucault: 'Why is struggle preferable to submission? Why ought domination to be resisted? Only with the introduction of some normative notions could he begin to tell us what is wrong with the modern power/knowledge regime and why we ought to oppose it.'

Poststructuralist critiques have been extremely useful in problematizing the 'subject' as constructed through language and in providing a vocabulary for feminists struggling with the limitations of earlier approaches. These insights might be usefully built upon and attention to the discursive construction of subjectivity and the plurality of subject positions need not mean that a material level of analysis is eschewed. This requires coupling deconstruction with reconstruction, and demands that we reconsider the positioning of essentialism versus nominalism as an either/or choice.

4.3.3 What is a woman? Essentialism versus nominalism reconsidered

The essentialism versus nominalism debate in feminist theory has been posed by Michele Barrett (1988b) as a continuum, with neither pole representing a satisfactory point of departure. Clearly gender cannot be treated in the manner of a Durkheimian social fact, with the acquisition of gender seen as the 'acquisition of a social identity that is already there' (p. 268). Yet neither, as Barrett goes on to point out, can we begin from the assumption that 'there is no such fixed social category already there but, rather, that the meaning of gender. . .is constructed anew in every encounter'. I think that the effectiveness of our theory and our politics rests not on finding some middle ground between these two poles, but by grasping both poles simultaneously, with all their contradictions. Paul Smith, in his study of the concept of the 'subject' in social theory, finds feminism paradigmatic in this respect, suggesting that 'By dint of this acceptation of the doubled nature of the "subject's" existence, feminism provides a view which counters the long and continuing history of (phallocratic) cerning[5] of the "subject" ' (1988: 152). This is exemplified by the work of Denise Riley, who suggests that '[I]nstead of veering between deconstruction and transcendence, we could try another train of speculation: that 'woman' is indeed an unstable category, that this instability has a historical foundation, and that feminism is the site of the systematic fighting-out of that instability' (1988: 5).

There is an inherent tension between the term 'woman' as a theoretical construct which implies gender as universally constitutive of the subject, and the realities of really existing 'women' who may or may not share a unified 'gender identity'. Recognizing this tension, it seems more appropriate to speak of 'gendered identities', implying a recognition of plurality and difference without abandoning the notion that gender does play a part in constituting the subject. It is precisely the conflict and the tension between the centred and decentred conceptions of the subject in feminist theory that contains the potential for theorizing resistive agency, on the part of both collective and individual subjects.

Another level of tension – that between gendered subjects and gendered structures – is also integral to developing feminist theory. Theorizing gender exclusively at the level of the subject risks letting social relations disappear from the realm of sexuality and gender, allowing gender to be seen as primarily located in the individual. This is one of the problems with psychoanalytic approaches. Gender is not only the psychic ordering of biological difference, it is also the social ordering of that difference. This point is neatly summarized by Paul Smith (1988: 77), who asserts that 'psychoanalytically informed explanations of the relationship between "subject" and other cannot be taken as if they were the last word in the theorizing of subjectivity, but always must be brought back round to a historicizing discussion of the ideologies and institutions (and thus the interests and practices) upon which subjectivity is predicated and which it serves'.

Clearly it is essential to retain an awareness of both levels if we are to grasp both domination and resistance. It is also essential to emphasize that not only women have a problematic relationship to gender thus construed. One of the consequences of the androcentric conception of the universal subject has been to obscure the fact that men, too, are gendered beings. Gender is, first and foremost, a relational concept. It is on this point that psychoanalytic and poststructuralist work has been most instructive. Yet these insights must be developed within a more explicitly sociological account of the negotiation of gendered identities.

At the social level, gender both describes and imposes an order on individuals. The gender order provides the 'mode of interpretation' through which individuals construct a subjective and social identity. As Seyla Benhabib (1987: 80) puts it, it is 'the grid through which the self develops an embodied identity, a certain mode of being in one's body and of living the body'; it is 'the grid through which societies and cultures reproduce embodied individuals'.

Thus, one of the key aspects of 'subjectivity', of 'consciousness', of 'identity' – be it classed, gendered, or raced – is coming to terms with, or learning to inhabit, one's body. This is not a project which 'ends' with the successful resolution of a predetermined set of 'stages', as the classical Freudian account would have it. Nor is it the basis for some unifying essence among those who share similar bodies, as certain feminist accounts would suggest. It is an ongoing process, a continual renegotiation of the relationship between self and others. It is both a 'sensual' and a cultural project which cannot be evaded through evocation of the 'autonomous' ego who somehow manages to transcend the bodily aspects of existence. Thus, not even the theoretically 'disembodied' male, who relies on the services of a subordinate female to mediate his relationship to his bodily needs, escapes a corporeally grounded existence. To have a relationship to one's body which is mediated by another does not eliminate the relationship, it only changes it. By challenging the mind/body dualism, feminism also challenges the historically prescribed relationship between culture and biology which contains their autonomy.

The opposition between autonomy and mutuality, or relatedness, must be subverted, to be seen as integral to the development of subjectivity. As Roslyn Bologh (1987: 151) suggests, 'The tension between a commitment to individual rights and a commitment to relationship must be maintained as a tension internal to moral reasoning itself'. The relationship between individual and society (or individual and community) must be seen at least partly as an internal tension, not totally externalized as classical theory has portrayed it. Thus the tension between public and private, political and personal, mind and body, masculine and feminine, must also be seen as an internal struggle in the construction of identities.

Drucilla Cornell and Adam Thurschwell (1987: 144), drawing on psychoanalytic and deconstructionist insights, suggest such an approach, arguing that 'gender categories themselves retain indelible traces of their Other, belying the rigid identification of one's self as a fully gender-differentiated subject'. This is not a new, more sophisticated concept of androgyny. Androgyny replicates, rather than subverts, the logic of gender polarity. Instead, the recognition of internally contradictory processes in the constitution of gendered identities recasts the Hegelian struggle for identity, suggesting that 'the dialectic of identity and difference plays itself out on the level of subjectivity as a construct' (Cornell and Thurschwell, 1987: 159). This poses a radically utopian challenge to essentialist formulations of gender polarity, in that essentialism 'misrepresents the self-difference of the gendered subject. It restricts the play of difference that marks every attempt to confirm identity' (p. 161). At the same time, it avoids the lapse into nominalism. It requires that we adopt a new vocabulary of difference which does not congeal into binary opposition.

4.4   Gendered Identities as Interpreted Identities

If my argument to this point holds, it is apparent that to begin to understand gender as relational, a new conception of the relationship between the individual and society — between subject and structure — must be forged. Reliance on historically abstracted dualisms — such as family/economy, male/female — as framing the individual/society relationship must give way to more fluid, historically nuanced conceptions of identity formation and subjectivity which do not fall back on the conflation of the gendered division of labour with the public/private dualism.

It is the recognition, and reclaiming, of the *tension* between individual and society, between subject and structure, that allows us to proceed in dialectical fashion in reconceptualizing gendered (or classed or raced) identities as relationally and historically *interpreted* — multiple, often contradictory, and actively constructed according to certain historically available modes of interpretation. Conceiving of identities as interpreted allows us to tread the precarious path between essentialism and nominalism and between agency and determination. To express in another way the two poles of the debate which need to be grasped simultaneously, the content of gender is infinitely variable and continually in flux, yet the salience of gender categories is persistent. It requires a recognition of the positioning of gendered subjects both materially and ideologically, yet always interpreted in terms of a gender polarity. It is on these grounds that we can explore how the social relations of domination embodied in gender polarity become invisible, personal and seemingly natural.

A number of useful conceptual tools for developing this sort of analysis of gender and of gendered subjectivities may be gleaned from recent feminist work. Matthews (1984) introduces the term 'gender order' to name the historically constructed web of power relations between men and women. She describes the gender order as a material and ideological grid, a system of power relations that 'turns barely differentiated babies into either women or men of the approved types, thereafter keeping them to the mark *as the definitions change*' [emphasis added]. Other orderings, such as race and class, 'cut across the gender order and deflect and modify it' (p. 13–14). It is in this complex of orderings that social meaning is created. To speak of a gender order is to speak of the manner in which sexual difference becomes social inequality — the 'building up' of differences into an ordering of relationships. At this level, it is an abstraction, and could be matriarchal, patriarchal or egalitarian in specific content.[6] Fleshing out the content of the gender order requires historical investigation, and a recognition that it is always in flux:

> The specific nature or content of any gender order is constantly in process, being formed and changed. It is fashioned by the actions of individuals who are themselves formed in that interaction. It is created in the struggles and power strategies and contradictions and unintended consequences of a multitude of social groups and individuals and interests. . . .The femininity and masculinity that are forged of these countervailing forces are never constant but always changing and, more often than not, internally inconsistent if not contradictory (Matthews, 1984: 14–15).

Thus, a gender order may be considered 'patriarchal' – that is, the masculine may be construed as dominant over the feminine – without lapsing into the transhistorical, agent-less conception of 'patriarchy'. A gender order begins with embodiment – the existence of males and females as inhabitants of different bodies and their self-awareness of such – and is elaborated through the historical construction of biological difference into essential psychological and social differences between women and men. As Matthews (1984: 16) summarizes it: 'Women as social beings are biological entities and self-aware identities who live within the strategies of prescription and punishment of the gender order.' So too, are men. It is the gender order, then, that provides the grid for regulating gendered identities, both materially and ideologically. However, we need a fuller account of the formation of gendered subjectivities in this configuration of power relations.

Alcoff (1988: 431) suggests that we need 'to construe a gendered subjectivity in relation to concrete habits, practices, and discourses while at the same time recognizing the fluidity of these'. Citing de Lauretis (1986) and Riley (1983) as exemplars of such an approach, what is suggested is 'a subjectivity that gives agency to the individual while at the same time placing her within "particular discursive configurations" and moreover, conceives of the process of consciousness as a strategy. Subjectivity may thus become imbued with race, class, and gender without being subjected to an overdetermination that erases agency' (Alcoff, 1988: 425).

As Burton (1985: 127) notes, the negotiation and construction of options is done from different vantage points, and some are more powerful than others. Alcoff (1988: 433) calls this 'positionality':

> When the concept 'woman' is defined not by a particular set of attributes but by a particular position, the internal characteristics of the person thus identified are not denoted so much as the external context within which that person is situated. The external situation determines the person's relative position, just as the position of a pawn on a chessboard is considered safe or dangerous, powerful or weak, according to its relation to the other chess pieces. . . .[This] makes her identity relative to a constantly shifting context, to a situation that includes a network of elements involving others, the objective economic conditions, cultural and political institutions and ideologies, and so on.

The notion of positionality is useful in drawing together both subjectivity and structure as they converge in the individual, and suggests that gender identity is not only relational to a given set of external conditions, but that 'the position women find themselves in can be actively utilized . . . as a place from where meaning is constructed, rather than simply the place from where a meaning can be discovered (the meaning of femaleness)' (Alcoff, 1988: 434). There is thus an incorporation of the insight derived from Foucault that power is not entirely negative. If we tie this back into Matthew's notion of a gender order, we have a starting point for understanding how knowledgeable, acting subjects may nonetheless tend to participate in the legitimation of the conditions which reproduce their 'position'.

The subject, then, is positioned in both the ideological and real senses. Fruitful lines of inquiry here would be to study how the discrepancy between the ideal and lived reality is experienced, and how our activity can at the same time support the reproduction of existing relations or be a factor of resistance.[7] Luxton captures this neatly in her follow-up study of women in Flin Flon, Manitoba. Women who were employed outside the home, yet held a traditional view of the 'proper' sphere for women 'were compelled to mediate the contradiction': 'Their attempts to defend a strict gendered division of labour forced them deeper into the double day. Their actual experiences highlight the conditions under which support for right-wing "pro-family" reform movements is generated, for in their opinion it is their paid work that creates the problem' (Luxton, 1990: 53).

Certainly much of the power of the New Right lies in its delineation of a relatively narrow set of acceptable subject-positions. As Stuart Hall (1988: 49) suggests in his analysis of Thatcherism, its power lies in being able to 'constitute new subject positions from which its discourses about the world make sense', to combine 'ideological elements into a discursive chain in such a way that the logic or unity of the discourse depends on the subject addressed assuming a number of specific subject positions'. The historically specific effectiveness of certain subject-positions in either legitimating or contesting such a discourse illustrates the futility of theorizing subjectivity as fixed in its relationship to social structure – an important charge against Marxist humanism, which has tended to posit 'an a priori historical subject or notion of agency on which revolution is premised' (Aronowitz, 1988: 523). This critique of Marxist humanism is equally instructive for feminism, which in its totalizing, essentialist moments has tended to replicate this error. Yet, accepting the deconstructionist notion that the constitution of the subject is simultaneously to constitute its subjection belies the potential for resistance that certain subject-positions embody. As a critique of Foucault comments: 'his peremptory equation of subjectification and subjection erases the distinction between the enforcement of compliance with a determinate system of norms, and the formation of a reflexive consciousness which may subsequently be directed in a critical manner against the existing system of norms' (Dews, cited in Soper, 1986: 139). Certain liberatory struggles (such as those on behalf of homosexuals or working mothers) could emerge only once their corresponding subject-positions or 'identities' were created.

The placing of subjects in certain subject-positions is a key mode of legitimation. Yet the liberatory potential lies in the fluid manner in which interests/identities are formed both within and across subject-positions. A key political task, then, is the articulation of interests in particular ways. As Connell (1987: 162) suggests: 'The definition of a married woman's interests as being essentially those of her husband and children is the hegemonic pattern; the definition of her interests as those of a group of exploited women in a factory is subversive.' Thus, the gender order, as a mode of interpretation, becomes a field of contestation over subject-positions, and contains the potential for 'crises of interest formation'.

4.5   The Politics of Gender Polarity

Against essentialist theories of gendered subjectivity and theories which ignore gender as constitutive of subjectivity altogether, I have focused on the multiple and often contradictory nature of subjectivity, and on the active construction of gendered identities in terms of historically available modes of interpretation.

Several points merit reiteration here. First, there is a need to reframe the individual/society relationship, inherited from the classical project, to recognize, not repress, the tension between internal and external forms of domination. Second, there is the need to recognize that part of that tension arises from the simultaneously social and individual project of constructing a seemingly unitary 'identity', or subjectivity, from a diverse web of positions which impose and in turn reproduce social interpretations of those positions. Third, it is necessary to build socialist feminist political strategies which take into account the partial and precarious nature of gendered identities, while at the same time recognizing their salience in constituting both individual subjectivities and social realities.

How then, do we reconcile the theoretical subject 'woman' with the really existing subjects called 'women'? This poses a key question for both theory and political practice. How do we negotiate the treacherous course of rejecting the fiction of 'woman' as a given category, while at the same time recognizing the need to fight for particular rights for 'women'? How do we avoid replicating and reinforcing the polarization of male/female that we criticize? Riley (1988: 112) argues that, 'it is compatible to suggest that "women" don't exist – while maintaining a politics of "as if they existed" – since the world behaves as if they unambiguously did'. We need to conceive of the social relations which make this paradox possible, *that exist as relations of unequal power*, as both inherited and re-created through their subjective inhabitation.

These relations are constructed and regulated through numerous practices – in the realms of labour, education, religion, language, media, jurisprudence, sexuality, just to name a few. If gendered identities are to be construed as interpreted identities, then the field of legitimation and (potentially) contestation of the gender order must be construed as one of identity politics. Any mode of interpretation through which identities are constructed is the result of contestation and resistance, allowing some interpretations and suppressing others. I will focus, in the next chapter, on the role of political discourse in regulating permissible identities, and thus as central to the mode of interpretation.

5

Gender Politics: Regulation and Resistance

Dominant socialist feminist theories of the production and reproduction of 'gender identity' and the resulting asymmetry of gender
relations have largely failed to take into account the conflictual and
contradictory character of those relations, tending to reify them in a
way which makes their regulation and reproduction relatively
unproblematic. Taking instead the perspective on gendered
identities as actively interpreted, multiple and often contradictory,
this chapter will build on several key areas of theory. First, I will
review feminist theories of the state, and sketch out a framework for
analysis which examines the regulation of gendered identities
embodied in the development of, and policies associated with,
modern welfare states. Drawing on theories of 'moral regulation',
which focus on the political regulation of permissible forms of
identity (Corrigan, 1990: Corrigan and Sayer, 1985; Kinsman,
1987; Valverde and Weir, 1988), I will suggest that the state, and
in particular the modern welfare state, does not just 'act' on
subjects, but actively constructs them in particular gendered, raced
and classed ways. The second body of theory that I want to build
on, and the focus of the latter part of the chapter, is concerned with
the emergence of a 'public sphere', in relation to the separation of
state and civil society in modernity, which may provide space
for the formation and constestation of identities (Calhoun, 1992;
Cohen and Arato, 1992; Felski, 1989a; Fraser, 1990; Fraser,

1992b; Habermas, 1989b; Habermas, 1992; Keane, 1984). Feminism as a social movement which seeks to reconfigure political discourse and create new identities figures prominently here.

5.1   Perspectives on the State

As Gramsci (1929–35/1971: 271) noted, 'every state tends to create and maintain a certain type of civilization and of citizen (and hence of collective life and of individual relations)'. As Corrigan and Sayer (1985) put it, 'States, if the pun be forgiven, state. They define in great detail, acceptable forms and images of social activity and individual and collective identity; they regulate, in empirically specifiable ways much. . .of social life.' States structure relationships and the parameters for interaction. Yet it is only within the last decade or so that the state has become central to feminist analysis. The tendency in earlier feminist work to separate out one institution – the family – as the primary bearer of gender relations deflected attention from seeing political practice itself as constituted by gender inequalities.

Connell (1987, 1990) suggests four views of the state that might be used to inform feminist work: liberal, Marxist, radical feminist and poststructuralist. None of these models in itself is adequate, yet in playing one off against the other, some valuable insights for theorizing the state and state policy may be gleaned.

The liberal view sees the state as a potentially neutral arbitrator, but one which has been captured by a particular interest group (in this case, men). As Connell suggests, this approach makes sense of the key demands of liberal feminism, and constitutes the grounds on which most of the gains of liberal feminism have been made – such as suffrage and other provisions for 'formal' equality. Significantly, it rests upon an uncritical acceptance of the liberal conception of individual rights, and fails to recognize the underlying logic of identity (difference equals duality) that perpetuates gender polarity. Thus, as Zillah Eisenstein has demonstrated in several works (1981, 1982, 1984, 1988), it belies its own critical potential in uncovering the manner in which the liberal rights discourse necessarily constructs women as 'not-men'.

The Marxist view treats the state as an instrument of class

domination, and sees it as entering into the regulation of gender relations as necessary to the reproduction of capitalism. Feminist work on the state which draws on this perspective has therefore concentrated on the state as a *capitalist* state. State activity regulating gender is tied to the requirements of capitalist production — maintaining women as a reserve army of labour, ensuring the reproduction of labour power, and so on. Theorists such as Varda Burstyn (1985) and Mary McIntosh (1978), for example, analyse 'state activity which supports the relations of male dominance specifically in terms of the capitalist accumulation process' (Randall, 1988: 11). This perspective tends not only towards reductionism, but accords a unity and purposive instrumental character to the state which it does not deserve. Debates within Marxism on the state (Jessop, 1982; Milliband, 1969; Poulantzas, 1978) have tended to be resolved *against* 'derivationism' — the assumption that the state can be derived from 'the capital form' (Pierson, 1984: 564).

The radical feminist view of the state is that it is inherently patriarchal. This perspective is represented most prominently by feminist legal theorist Catharine MacKinnon, for whom state power is male power. MacKinnon turns Marxism 'inside out and on its head': 'Feminism stands in relation to marxism as marxism does to classical political economy: its final conclusion and ultimate critique' (1982: 30). The state, represented by legal 'objectivity', is the institutionalization of the male point of view, of male power. Yet as Valverde and Weir (1988: 31) conclude, from this perspective the class reductionism of Marxism is 'quietly transformed into an equally totalizing gender reductionism' which sees all forms of regulation as 'explainable by reference to male interests'.

The poststructuralist view of the state is that it represents 'part of a dispersed apparatus of social control working through dominant discourses as well as force' (Connell, 1987: 130), but that it is not inherently anchored in any particular economic-class or sex-class interest. That is, interests, identity and privilege are constructed anew in particular discursive articulations. Both the work of Foucault and that of Laclau and Mouffe (1985) are illustrative here.

Foucault radically de-centres the state, refusing to recognize any unity of power as it appears in particular institutionalized hierarchies such as state forms, or any continuity of privilege across locations. We should, insists Foucault (1980: 97–8), 'try to locate power at the extreme points of its exercise, where it is always less legal in character. . . .Power must be analyzed as something which circulates. . . .It is never localized here or there, never in anybody's hands'. The modern state, for Foucault, represents both an 'individualizing and a totalizing form of power' (1981: 782): that is, it is not something which exists *over* individiuals, but is 'a very sophisticated structure, in which individuals can be integrated, under one condition: that this individuality would be shaped in a new form and submitted to a set of very specific patterns' (783). This grounds the important work conducted by Foucault, and those influenced by him, on the surveillance and regulatory effects of the modern state. Yet he never explicitly reconnects the dispersions of power and the simultaneous individualizing/totalizing effects to existing hierarchies of class, race and gender as they are represented by modern states.[1]

The approach adopted by Laclau and Mouffe (1985) also de-centres the state, replacing it with a pluralistic conception of power relations. The state, as a 'centre' of the social is rendered implausible, as are Marxist debates about its 'relative autonomy' (1985: 139–41). While this tack might encourage recognition of newly emerging political subjects, and is equally appealing in its assertion that the state represents only the 'construction of a political space which can only be the result of hegemonic articulations' (p. 140), it obscures the whole question of state power as we experience it. Laclau's and Mouffe's theoretical strategy rests on an appropriation and development of Gramsci's concept of hegemony, but in their hands, it becomes severed from any anchoring in identifiable class or gender interests. Gramsci (1929–35/1971: 377) stressed that structures and superstructures form an historic bloc 'in which precisely material forces are the content and ideologies are the form, though this distinction between form and content has purely didactic value, since the material forces would be inconceivable historically without form and the ideologies would be individual fancies without the material forces'. By severing the concept of hegemony from a material grounding, Laclau and Mouffe give us form without content.

The perspective that I wish to outline here is one that takes the state as both an empirical and ideological configuration, played out at the level of institutional forms. From the liberal model, I will take the ideology of 'equality' as fundamental to the legitimation of these forms, but suggest, contra liberalism, that within the rhetoric of equality there are a variety of terms in which claims for equality may be pressed, or sometimes, *sup*pressed. From the Marxian model, I accept that state forms are integral to the economic project of capitalism, but contra Marxism, will suggest that the crucial space for analysis is in the 'autonomous' moments of the state. As Aronowitz (1981, 2/1990: 242) puts it, 'it is in the moment of autonomy, rather than the moment of dependence upon corporate capital, that [the state] reveals its sustained power to erect a system of beliefs, myths and symbols that can be successfully integrated into social consciousness'. From the radical feminist model, it must be granted that the state is patriarchal – although not inherently so. Rather it is patriarchal in character as a result of particular historical struggles. Within the institutional configuration of the state, 'patriarchy is both constructed and contested' (Connell, 1987: 130). Finally, from poststructuralism, there is no doubt that the state, through certain discourses, is implicated in processes of surveillance and regulation, and this perspective introduces an institutional level of analysis which is essential to a de-centred approach to the state. Yet in the recognition of plurality, it is sometimes too easy to lose sight of inequality. It is necessary to reintegrate into this de-centred view of the state and political discourse the notion of *interests* (economic, sexual, moral) if we are to find viable ground for a liberatory politics.

In a brilliant article on the difficulties of studying the state, Abrams (1988) suggests that the key task in the study of the state is the understanding and exposure of the way in which the state is constructed as an 'illusory general interest' (Marx and Engels, 1845–6/1970: 54). Given the feminist critique of the historical and philosophical exclusion of women from 'humanity', the notion of an 'illusory general interest' takes on especial significance. It has been noted that the state-system must present the impression of a 'unity of interests to maintain its legitimacy as the representative of the people, as opposed to the representative of class and gender interests' (Sue Findlay, cited in Barnsley, 1988: 19).

Abrams (1988: 80–2) suggests that we need two objects of study – the state-system and the state-idea. The state-system is that 'palpable nexus of practice and institutional structure centred in government'. The state-idea is that 'ideological artifact' attributing unity, morality and independence to the disunited, amoral and dependent workings of the practice of government. It is folly, he suggests, to suppose that we also have to study 'the state' as 'an entity, agent, function or relation over and above the state-system and state-idea'[2]:

> In sum: the state is not the reality which stands behind the mask of political practice. It is itself the mask which prevents our seeing political practice as it is. . . .The ideological function is extended to a point where conservatives and radicals alike believe that their practice is not directed at each other but at the state; the world of illusion prevails (1988: 82).

The idea of the state is constructed out of the state-system, in what Jenson (1987: 65) terms the 'universe of political discourse'. The universe of political discourse draws the lines between public and private, and sets the parameters of political action by limiting 'the range of actors that are accorded the status of legitimate participants, the range of issues considered to be included within the realm of meaningful political debate; the policy alternatives feasible for implementation; the alliance strategies available for achieving change'. In the end, the most important effect of the realm of political discourse at any point in time 'is to inhabit or encourage the formation of new collective identities and/or the reinforcement of older ones.' (p. 65).

Countless studies of state policies — whether expressed through welfare programmes, laws, educational institutions, interventions in the labour market, family policies, or numerous other manifestations — conclude that state actions affect the ways in which 'feminine and masculine lives are constructed' (Jenson, 1986: 9). Yet while such observation suggests that the state activity *does* contribute to the constitution of the categories of the gender order, 'observation of such effects does not constitute any explanation of *why* they exist' (p. 10). Such an explanation is best sought, not with abstract reference to the 'needs of capital' or the 'interests of patriarchy', but in an examination of specific practices through which the parameters for gendered identities are both constructed and potentially become sites of resistance. As Corrigan (1990: 121) reminds us: 'We live in worlds which are as much moral as material, indeed there is no way of appropriating and handling the material which does not involve forms of expression some of which carry a higher evaluation than others'. Just as the creation of 'moral subjects' was (is) essential to state formation (Corrigan and Sayer, 1985; Valverde and Weir, 1988), so is the creation of those subjects as properly gendered.

While the state is often taken to be the agent of moral regulation, this focus tends to obscure 'the complex relationships among state and non-state institutions involved in developing and reproducing codes of moral regulation' (Valverde and Weir, 1988: 31). Regulation here does not equal simply reactive measures necessary to maintain the social order. Regulation functions not only through direct control, but by 'defining the parameters and content of choice, fixing how we come to want what we want' (Henriques et al., 1984: 219). This is particularly true for liberal democracies which, at least on a rhetorical level, reject coercion as a means to secure order. It is important, then, to examine not only the state, but different forces in the broader arena of political discourse.

5.2 Policy as Interpretation and Regulation

State activity implicated in the regulation of gendered identities is dispersed over a range of institutional sites. Some institutions and policies are explicitly gendered, for example provisions governing maternity leave. Bhavnani and Coulson (1986: 84) remind us as well of the manner in which racism 'places different women in different relationships to structures of authority'; the state 'deals with different women differently'. This is most obvious in the case of immigration policy and related legislation (Arat-Koç, 2/1990), but is also evident in employment policies (Ng, 1988), the criminal justice system (Diaz-Cotto, 1991; Samuelson and Marshall, 1991), and in the delivery of health, education and social services. Through these dispersed activities, state subjects are constituted and regulated in both gender- and race-specific ways. In most cases, however, this regulation is not explicit, but implicit – disguised by supposedly neutral categories such as tax-payer, worker, dependant, client, recipient, citizen, consumer and the ubiquitous 'family'. Balbo (1987: 204) goes so far as to suggest that the very emergence of the modern state might be understood as occurring through a 'process of establishing, shifting and redefining boundaries between state and individual via the family'.

There is no denying that the family remains crucial to feminist struggle. As Morgan (1985: 254–6) notes, it is 'the point to which, however labyrinthine, the paths always return':

> [T]he family is both societal and individual, both institutional and personal, both public and private. . . .[T]he very terms which are used in the analysis — family, marriage, parenthood — themselves have a history, a socially constructed character and. . .terms such as mother and father, husband and wife are both at one and the same time institutional and individual.

This is not to suggest, as I have criticized much feminist theory for doing, that we should pick out one institution — the family — as the 'bearer' of gender, leaving the rest untheorized. Nor will I suggest that there is 'a' family about which we can speak.[3] As Luxton (1987: 238) summarizes it, the family exists in two distinct but interrelated forms: as 'familialism', 'a widespread and deeply embedded ideology about how people ought to live' and as 'economic and social groups which in fact organize domestic and personal life'. Families and the ideology of familialism are absolutely central to women's history and the regulation of gender. The family, above all else, has long been the site of conflicting interests and demands on the state from a range of constituencies.

Procreation itself must be seen as a political activity. At the most basic level, it is through the bearing of children that society is kept alive. But the rearing of those children is equally important. As Vickers (1987: 485) notes: 'Nationalism, tribalism, ethnicity and most religions work through the reproductive mode. Our mother tongue and what we learn at our mother's knee shape to a considerable degree what identity we will adopt, what group we will be loyal to and what authority figures we will accept as legitimate.' It is no surprise, then, that the state has an interest in this most gendered of activities.

The last century in most Western nations has been characterized by what Foucault terms a 'bio-politics of the population', a concern with the *species* body – 'the body imbued with the mechanics of life and serving as the basis of the biological processes: propagation, births and mortality, the level of health, life expectancy and longevity' (Foucault, 1976/1978: 139). To be sure, the requirements of capitalist economies for a supply of relatively healthy labourers influenced this discourse, but it cannot be reduced to this. Population politics, as Matthews (1984: 75) suggests, have been characterized by a range of 'overlapping and shifting' interests – religious, scientific, class-political, race-political and gender-political. Thus, both state and non-state groups and agencies engaged in debate around 'population ideology', which, in the late 19th and early 20th centuries, generally held that 'a large, healthy and "racially pure" population was central to moral and economic progress' (Matthews, 1984: 74). As she concludes, the central focus of population politics was women's bodies: 'its principle mode of control was women's work within their families; its central icon was the Ideal Mother' (p. 75).

While the construction of population ideology in most Western nations was dispersed over a range of sites (for example, immigration, education, public health and welfare policies, medicine), the 'Ideal Mother', as the bearer and rearer of a moral citizenry was at the centre of debate.

Decreasing birth rates and increasing labour market participation among women did little to change their position in political discourse as mothers. Even the effects of the Second World War, widely hailed as a watershed for the women in nations such as Britain, the United States and Canada, did not significantly resolve the opposition between worker and mother. Women were essential to the war effort – as military personnel, civilian industrial workers, agricultural workers, volunteers and careful consumers. Women responded to the opportunities available and governments responded to the need for their labour. But they were not, even after all of this, workers – they were *women* workers. Hence the post-war retrenchment in most nations: day nurseries lost their funding; marriage bars dropped back into place in the civil service; pro-natalist policies were introduced (Riley, 1983). As Pierson (1983: 26–7) summarizes it, 'the sexual division of labour reemerged stronger than ever' and 'the dominant message was that women's chief function was to bear and rear the next generation'.

Although women's labour market participation rates never dropped to their pre-war levels, during the post-war period there was a retrenchment of the maternal ideal. Again, this was by no means an unproblematic imposition of the will of the state on women – while state policy certainly encouraged women to move from the work-place back to the home, the maternal ideal was also constructed through the economy, which promoted domestic consumption, and through academia and the media, which popularized theories such as Bowlby's 'maternal deprivation' thesis (Riley, 1983) and constructed the 'working mother' as a social problem. The very term 'working mother' brought together two formerly disparate identities (worker, mother) – never disparate in material reality, but disparate in the dominant ideological discourse, including that of the social sciences. Eventually, as the economy increasingly depended on the availability of women's labour – it became a new, permissible (though somewhat problematic) subject-position, specifically feminine. It remains a key site of contestation in political discourse around gender.

In most nations where influential feminist movements have emerged, anti-feminist movements have also become powerful social forces, and the family figures centrally in their politics. Demands are made on the state both to respect the 'privacy' of the family unit (for example, by giving parents the sole right to teach sex education) and simultaneously to intervene by protecting the patriarchal family (for example, by legislating a 'family wage'). In other words, the state is being called upon to protect the gendered division of labour as essential to the protection of a private sphere. Their strategy, like that of neoconservative movements more generally, is to 'restore the nonpolitical, noncontingent and uncontestable foundations of civil society (such as property, the market, the work ethic, the family)' (Offe, 1985: 820).

Real implications for feminist theory and practice lie in the fact that gender polarity has been mystified via the invocation of 'equality'. The rhetoric of the New Right is illuminating in its interpretation of the relationship between the public and the private (here, the state and the family), the conflation of this with the sexual division of labour, and the potential for a legitimation crisis in the state as regulator of the gender order. For the anti-feminist right, the family is seen as the basic unit of society, a 'natural' unit which is before the state. We cannot, however, confuse their demands for family privacy with the call for a general protection of privacy in personal life, for at the same time the state is being urged to withdraw from intervention in the 'family', it is being called on to increase its surveillance of 'other' populations (homosexuals, immigrants, welfare recipients). The 'family' here is specifically the white family headed by a male, and this is what is threatened by feminism. Anti-feminism operates in a space opened by feminism ('the personal is the political') and has fashioned an agenda which purports to address the real needs of women in a way that feminism has not.

As Campbell (1987: 151–2) notes in Britain, 'Conservative ideology is increasingly concerned with the idea of the family rather than the *work* of motherhood'. The family becomes central in the defence of the *individual* – against the state, and in particular against what is perceived as the creeping socialism of the welfare state. Brigette and Peter Berger (1983) wrote an influential academic version of this argument, which represents a sociological defence of the bourgeois family that ties together the psychological, economic and political implications of familial ideology. Their argument is built upon the assumption that maternal nurturance is essential to the development of autonomous (read male) individuals, asserting that 'the family, and specifically the bourgeois family, is the necessary social context for the emergence of the autonomous individuals who are the empirical foundation of political democracy' (1983: 186). They conclude that when 'family obligations come to be perceived as obstacles to self-realization in (women's) careers, individual women will have to decide on their priorities. Our own hope is that many will come to understand that life is more than a career and that this "more" is above all to be found in the family. But, however individual women decide, they should not expect public policy to underwrite and subsidize their life plans' (p. 205). In other words, the very foundation of democracy rests upon the devotion of women to the nurturance of children, and to encourage them to pursue other interests (for example, by providing public funds for day-care centres) is counter to the 'greater good'. This is not a new argument – it is a restatement, albeit in sophisticated academic terms, of the essential gender polarity which has prompted the regulation of procreation and the drive to produce a moral citizenry which has characterized most policy intervention into 'the family' (read women). Thus, the family is deployed as the necessary precondition for authority, private property, morality, and the general stability of society. The family becomes paired against a range of oppositions: the family versus drug abuse, the family versus homosexuality, the family versus the state, the family versus feminism. For the New Right, the 'family' is above history (Campbell, 1987: ch. 7) and above all, the woman as mother is the cornerstone of the family. Yet as Kessler-Harris (1988: 248–9) comments, it is an argument, which like much social policy, "invents a history" which ignores both the diversity of women's experiences and the struggles over their regulation. Current political discourse around 'family values'[4] harks back to the moral panics over suffrage in the US, where cartoons proliferated in the late nineteenth and early twentieth centuries depicting women's suffrage as inevitably followed by their wearing suits and smoking cigars while neglected children cried as their harried and de-masculinized fathers attempted to tend to them (Franzen and Ethiel, 1988). The 'war over the family' (the phrase used by Berger and Berger as the title of their book, 1983) is at its root a debate over gendered identities. The regulation of social identities, as they are constructed on the exclusion of certain particularities from the universal public sphere of rights is integral to the development of the modern welfare state.

5.3   Gender and the Welfare State

Taken broadly, the term 'welfare state' indicates a state form which embodies interventions into the market economy to take some responsibility for the well-being of its citizens. While there is no single model of 'the' welfare state, features common to all include some notion of social citizenship or moral equality as the basis of its legitimacy, and some commitment by the state to tempering the excesses of capitalism, by direct restraint of the market and/or provision of services to compensate for market inequities. In both these aspects, the development of the welfare state has embodied a continual redrawing of lines between public and private, between state and civil society, and in particular, between state, market and family. Women have never been merely the passive subjects of this development, but have been integrally and differentially connected to the welfare state since its earliest inception. Historical and comparative research demonstrates that women's reform efforts were instrumental in the emergence of modern welfare states. Women were often the first to identify and respond to the welfare needs of women and children and to argue for state welfare programmes (Koven and Michel, 1990).

The manner in which gender divisions were crucial in bringing about the welfare state is often obscured by the emphasis on the 'utopia of social labour' which fuelled its vision (Habermas, 1989a). That is, the bulk of analyses have focused on the degree to which welfare states have secured the reproduction of the labour force through varying degrees of the 'de-commodification' of labour. Offe (1984: 148), for example, suggests that:

> Social democratic reformism, Christian socialism, enlightened conservative political and economic elites, and large industrial unions were the most important forces which fought for and conceded more and more comprehensive compulsory insurance schemes, labour protection legislation, minimum wages, the expansion of health and education facilities, and state subsidized housing.

Yet, in accounts such as this, the 'reproduction of the labour force', although the focus of what defines the welfare state, is insufficiently deconstructed into its gendered aspects. But perhaps more importantly, an emphasis on the de-commodification of labour as the bedrock of the welfare state deflects attentions from the *moral* project of the welfare state. Distinctly gendered roles of citizen, worker and client begin to emerge as shaping the relationship of the state to its populace.

The growth of welfare state services has raised new questions around entitlement and has put the concept of citizenship at the centre of both political and theoretical agendas.[5] As Gordon (1990b: 173) notes, while the growing body of scholarship on the welfare state understands it 'to reflect and form the class system', gender as a category of analysis has not been central. If we consider that the earliest developments of the welfare state occurred when women were not yet formally citizens, and the continuing manner in which the roles of citizen and worker stand in opposition to that of woman, then it becomes clear that women and men have been incorporated into the social citizenry of the welfare state in distinctly different ways (Pateman, 1988: 231). Liberal conceptions of citizenship, such as that in the classic account of T.H. Marshall (1950), see women's rights as part and parcel of the inevitable extension of citizenship to an increasingly wider circle of individuals. What this account fails to capture is the manner in which the exclusion of some groups from citizenship has been, from the start, integral to the entitlement of other groups. For example, men were entitled to citizenship not just as individuals, but 'in their capacity as members and representatives of a family (i.e. a group of non-citizens)' (Ursula Vogel, cited in Yuval-Davis, 1991: 63). Furthermore, Marshall's periodization of the evolution of citizenship rights is faulty. As Gordon (1990b: 178) summarizes the feminist critique: 'His stages of citizenship (first due process rights, then political rights, or the franchise, then social citizenship or welfare entitlements) only describe the male experience; throughout the world women won important "social" rights from the state before they got the vote. Indeed, for many poor women, the earliest relation to the state was as a recipient of relief.'

Women's relationship to the welfare state has always been, and remains, contradictory. At the same time that it has regulated and shaped the gender-specific parameters of social life, the welfare state has provided a basis for women's social citizenship. This paradoxical relationship of women to the welfare state is strengthened as the latter comes under attack – the women's movement has, as Banting (1987: 318) puts it, emerged as 'one of the political bulwarks of the social role of the state'. Few feminists, despite their criticisms, would wish to see the welfare state dismantled.

The idea of the welfare state, centred on the abstract issues of citizenship and equality, inevitably raises questions of equality versus difference, and of inclusion and exclusion. As Scott (1988: 172) suggests, we need to be aware of the gender-political dimensions of this debate: 'when equality and difference are paired dichotomously, they structure an impossible choice. If one opts for equality, one is forced to accept the notion that difference is antithetical to it. If one opts for difference, one admits that equality is unattainable.' This is a playing out, at the political level, of the familiar opposition of universal and particular. Conventional theories of citizenship and individual 'rights' rest upon notions of formal justice, which is based on the autonomous individual, detached from any particularities and disassociated from 'interests'. But this non-particular individual upon which formal justice relies is particular — he is male, white, heterosexual and economically privileged.

Fraser (1989) illustrates the regulation of gendered social identities in an analysis of US social welfare policies. While such programmes as Unemployment Insurance and Social Assistance are presumably constructed on a gender-neutral model of individual rights, a feminist reading finds a two-tiered system. On the one hand, there are programmes geared to individuals, usually tied to participation in the labour force (such as Unemployment Insurance), and for whom the majority of beneficiaries are male. Benefits in these programmes are generally based upon entitlement criteria — such as number of weeks worked. On the other hand, there are programmes geared to households, such as welfare, 'designed to compensate for family failures, generally the absence of a male breadwinner' (Fraser, 1989: 149). The majority of beneficiaries of these programmes are female. Female beneficiaries of distributive policies are positioned not as citizens bearing rights, but as needy 'clients'. They are subject to more surveillance and therapeutic intervention. The benefits are distributed *from* an individualized public (tax-payers) *to* a relationally defined set of consumers. As Connell (1987: 132) suggests, women are more generally constructed as 'consumers' of state services as someone's mother, wife, ex-wife or widow. Thus, they are deviations from the ideal of the autonomous 'citizen', revealing the pervasive masculinity of that seemingly neutral being. Men are individuals, women are related to individuals.

The gender polarity of dependence versus autonomy reverberates throughout public policy, and (in the public realm) is explicitly entrenched in the political agenda of encouraging (in the public realm) increased individual self-reliance and relegation of caring to the private — to be done, not surprisingly, by women. As Jessica Benjamin (1988: 201) notes:

[T]he moment women take advantage of the logic of universality. . .the advocates of autonomy trot out the hidden gender clause. The unspoken assumption is that women, by upholding the private sphere and creating a nurturing environment, create the framework for the autonomous individuality of men.

Thus, gender polarity is, in the sense that Jenson (1989: 74) uses the term, a 'hegemonic paradigm': 'a set of interconnected premises which make sense of, or give meaning to, many social relations. . . .[I]t constitutes a kind of explanation of the world at the level of common sense as well as in formal theory.' Within this paradigm, 'acceptable forms and images of social activity and individual and collective identities' are defined (Corrigan and Sayer, 1985: 4). Clearly, policies become 'institutionalized patterns of interpretations' (Fraser, 1989: 156). At the same time, they obscure their normative assumptions and the gender polarity of autonomy and nurturance which constitute them. Thus, a 'particular moral order' is presented as description (Corrigan and Sayer, 1985: 6), suppressing alternative interpretations and giving the illusion that this is the only permissible interpretation.

The organization of gender difference, cross-cut by race and class, and regulated through the construction of various legal, social and economic boundaries between public and private is integral to the moral project of the state. As Valverde and Weir (1988: 31–2) caution, however, 'The public/private distinction operates as a complex regulatory strategy organizing multiple "realms" which in practice do not remain separate.' The very development of the welfare state has been a redrawing of boundaries, opening to public scrutiny and debate matters previously confined to privacy, and raising new questions about the relationship between state and civil society.

5.4　Revitalizing the Public Sphere?

In his introduction to *Civil Society and the State*, John Keane (1988) outlines three important ways in which the state–civil society schema may be understood: as an analytic device, used for explanatory purposes; as the basis of a political strategy, serving as the 'criterion to establish what must be done (and what must not be done) in order to reach a goal whose desirability is taken for granted' (p. 21); and as a springboard for normative questions. These distinctions are not entirely separable from one another, but they do tend to raise questions about what the *goals* are for critical theory and practice. This is particularly applicable to the normative dimension, which I therefore wish to pursue in the remainder of this chapter. Some of the most promising contributions to theorizing the state/civil society distinction in these terms have come from feminists grappling with the tension between the particular and the universal as it might ground the revitalization of autonomous public spheres. It is useful to locate this project in the broader questions of the potential and problems of modernity as elaborated by Hegel and Marx, and as reformulated by Habermas.

For Hegel, the creation of civil society, that space which stood between the patriarchal family and the state, is 'the achievement of the modern world' (Hegel, 1821/1967: 266–7). Civil society was a novel category of the social, based on the two principles of the 'concrete person' and 'universality' (pp. 122–3), or more specifically, founded in the reconciliation of particular needs of concrete persons with principles of universality (pp. 126–8). Thus, Hegel's concept of this unique domain of the social (civil society) rests on the concrete (male) person, liberated from the constraints of traditional authority, free to pursue his particular interests. Hegel recognized well the destructive potential of unrestrained particularity, and stressed the need to order it politically on the principles of universality, represented by the state. The unity of concrete (particular) and abstract (universal) individuality was to be found in the state.

The young Marx also recognized the emergence of civil society as a historical event, and recognized the achievement of the 'bourgeois revolution' in setting free 'the political spirit, which had. . .been dissolved, fragmented and lost in the various culs-de-sac of feudal society' (Marx, 'On the Jewish Question' [1844], in Tucker, 2/1978: 45). Marx recognized the necessity of the uncoupling of economic and political statuses for the development of capitalism, but the formal 'freedom' of civil society was rooted in the substantive 'unfreedom' of the capitalist market. The state, far from being the ethical unity of Hegel's formulation, can only secure this illusion. In the suppression of distinctions such as rank and property, the state presupposes them, allowing them to 'act after their own fashion. . .to manifest their particular nature'. Thus, the political state, for Marx, divests us of our 'real, individual' lives, and infuses us with an 'unreal universality'. 'Political emancipation certainly represents a great progress. It is not, indeed, the final form of human emancipation, but it is the final form of human emancipation *within* the framework of the prevailing social order' (p. 35). Against Hegel, Marx sees political emancipation as at best partial — true emancipation (what he terms 'true democracy', rather than socialism, in his early writings) can only be achieved by *overcoming* the distinction between civil society and the political state. That is, the unification of particular and universal, the achievement of concrete individuality as opposed to the illusory, abstract individuality of bourgeois civil society, rests in the unity of social and political life. While Marx (correctly) recognizes Hegel's version of individuality as an abstraction, he is no less successful in reconciling the abstract with the concrete through his strategy of collapsing civil society into the capitalist market. As Whitebook (1981: 90) notes: '[he] 'cannot move beyond the abstract individuality of bourgeois society. The promissory note for a concept of concrete individuality remains unredeemed.'

If there has been one connecting between which ties together Habermas's early and late work, it is the concept of 'public space', rooted in the Enlightenment notion of reason, as both a historical category and a normative category. Habermas criticizes both Hegel and Marx for failing to see the irreversible gains embodied in the emergence of the bourgeois public sphere. Hegel, he says, 'took the teeth out of the idea of the public sphere' by seeking to integrate citizens into the state 'from above', thereby sacrificing the potential of participatory democracy (Habermas, 1962/1989b: 120–2). Marx, on the other hand, erred in seeing the bourgeois public sphere as 'mere ideology', and in seeing the dissolution of civil society as precursor to real emancipation (pp. 123–9). Habermas's project must be seen as one which tries to develop a model of the relationship between civil society and the state which avoids both Hegel's 'integration from above' and Marx's reductionism to class dynamics, yet does not retreat behind their considerable insights. As Hohendahl (1979: 104) notes, Habermas's early work on the public sphere constituted a 'first attempt to introduce, within the

notions of rational discourse, a concept of communicative interaction'. Habermas (1962/1989b: 27) summarizes his analysis of the
emergence and disintegration of the 'public' as a *category* of
bourgeois society as follows:

> The bourgeois public sphere may be conceived above all as the
> sphere of private people come together as a public; they soon
> claimed the public sphere regulated from above against the public
> authorities themselves, to engage them in a debate over the general
> rules governing relations in the basically privatized but publicly
> relevant sphere of commodity exchange and social labour. The
> medium of this political confrontation was peculiar and without
> historical precedent: people's public use of their reason.

Theoretically this public sphere was open to all – practically, it was
dominated by the male, educated, property-owning class – and
while never fully realized as the sphere of formation of a fully
generalized interest, the potential of communicatively secured
decision making (as opposed to that which is normatively secured,
via reference to traditional worldviews) which it engendered has
remained central to Habermas's work. The bourgeois values of
universal civil rights continue to exert influence in advanced
capitalism, so that 'legitimation can be disassociated from the
mechanism of elections only temporarily and under extraordinary
conditions' (Habermas, 1973/1975: 36). Yet substantive democracy, or 'genuine participation in the processes of political will-
formation' would expose the 'contradiction between administrat-
ively socialized production and the continued private appropriation
and use of surplus value'. To avoid this sort of crisis requires a
legitimation process that generates loyalty without genuine
participation: 'This structural alteration of the bourgeois public
realm. . .provides for application of institutions and procedures
that are democratic in form, while the citizenry, in the midst of an
objectively political society, enjoy the status of passive citizens with
only the right to withhold acclamation' (p. 37). Yet the potential
for a revitalized public sphere, embodying truly rational and
democratic 'will formation' via 'universal pragmatics', is the *raison
d'être* for Habermas's theory of communicative action. It requires a
'counterfactual reconstruction', asking (p. 113):

how would members of a social system. . .have collectively and
bindingly interpreted their needs (and which norms would they have
accepted as justified) if they could and would have decided on
organization of social intercourse through discursive will formation,
with adequate knowledge of the limiting conditions and functional
imperatives of their society?

Habermas (1976/1979: 186) reiterates the potential for a revitalized
public in terms of a learning process:

> I can imagine the attempt to arrange a society democratically only as
> a self-controlled learning process. It is a question of finding
> arrangements which can ground the presumption that the basic
> institutions of the society and the basic political decisions would
> meet with the unforced agreement of all those involved, if they
> could participate, as free and equal, in discursive will-formation.

In a later work, Habermas (1981/1987a: 329) reaffirms his belief in
the unexhausted potential of the ideological and structural changes
wrought by modernity:

> To be sure, the utopia of reason, formed in the Enlightenment was
> persistently contradicted by the realities of bourgeois life. . . .But
> it was never a mere illusion. . . .To the extent that culture, society
> and personality separated off from one another. . .and the validity
> basis of communicative action replaced the sacred foundations of
> social interaction, there was at least an appearance of posttraditional
> everyday communication suggested by the structures of the
> lifeworld. . . .In it communication was represented as dynamics of
> autonomous subsystems, bursting encapsulated expert cultures and
> thus as escaping the combined threat of reification and desolation.

The one-sided instrumentalization of reason has blocked the
potential of the communicative infrastructure, 'burying alive'
possibilities for expression (Habermas, 1981/1987a: 395). The task
of critical theory is that of recovering this potential. The concept of
the public sphere, and the potential of its revitalization, provides,
for Habermas, a means whereby he can recognize the advances of the
bourgeois revolution without having to rest a defence of these gains
on Hegel's statism or Marx's prescription of collapsing the public/

private distinction. Yet what is unclear for feminists is whether, as Landes (1988: 202) puts it, we can simply ' "take possession" of a public sphere that has been enduringly reconstructed along masculinist lines'.

As Fraser (1990) suggests, Habermas's conceptualization of a public sphere improves upon both earlier Marxist accounts, which tend to conflate 'public' with 'state', and feminist formulations which tend to refer to anything outside the domestic sphere as 'public'. While we can thus agree that 'something like Habermas's idea of the public sphere is indispensable to critical social theory and to democratic political practice', Fraser's examination of other, 'revisionist' accounts of the emergence of the bourgeois public sphere suggest that 'the specific form in which Habermas has elaborated this idea is not entirely satisfactory' (p. 57). Specifically, she finds his focus on a universalist bourgeois public both historically inaccurate, in that it leads him to ignore other sorts of publics which have always existed alongside and conflicted with bourgeois publics, and undesirable as a normative model, in that it underplays the manner in which such a public was 'a masculinist ideological notion that functioned to legitimate an emergent form of class rule' (p. 62). A more adequate theorization would include attention to *multiple* publics and to the manner in which social inequalities structure *differential access* to publicity. This requires not the bracketing of status differentials, but their explicit thematization (p. 64). Against Habermas's universalist aspirations, this means thematizing a diversity of interests as 'public' in such a way that they are not dismissed as 'illegitimate particularisms' (Leonard, 1990: 244).

Fraser (1990) has begun to develop a 'socialist-feminist critical theory of late capitalist political culture' focusing on the politics of need interpretation. The model she develops, which theorizes the 'sociocultural means of interpretation and communication', owes a considerable debt to Habermas. By the 'sociocultural means of interpretation and communication' she refers to 'the historically and culturally specific ensemble of discursive resources available to members of a given social collectivity in pressing claims against one another' (1989: 164). These resources include the 'officially recognized idioms in which one can press claims' (for example, in terms of needs, rights, interests), the 'vocabularies' available within these idioms (for example, therapeutic, administrative, religious, feminist or socialist), the 'paradigms of argumentation accepted as authoritative' (for example, scientific, legal, political), the conventions available for constructing individual and collective identities, and 'modes of subjectification', or the 'ways in which various discourses position the people to whom they are addressed as specific sorts of subjects' (e.g. as 'normal' or 'deviant'). Fraser extends Habermas's insights in that, first, she recognizes (to a greater extent than he seems to) the discursive arena of society is stratified in terms of a number of axes of domination (class, gender, race, etc.). Second, she is more sensitized to the different ways in which issues are quite fluidly politicized and de-politicized as public/private boundaries constantly shift. Third, she recognizes the manner in which the discourse over 'needs' is crucial in the constitution of new collective identities (1989: 172):

> For example. . .groups of women have politicized and reinterpreted various needs, have instituted new vocabularies and forms of address, and so, have become 'women' in a different, though not uncontested or univocal sense.

The importance of addressing issues of identity formation through an analysis of historically available options is clearly crucial for feminist theory.

Fraser also takes an important step beyond Habermas's procedural emphasis to highlight the importance of the *consequences*, for different groups, of the outcome of needs interpretations. As an instructive example, she works through the discourse around wife-battering, from its politicization by feminists, and its importance through a politics of 'need interpretation' in the creation of new public spaces for consciousness-raising, to its translation into a question of administrative need-satisfaction, in such a way as to individualize and de-politicize the issue. Similar conclusions have been reached on the basis of feminist analyses of pay equity (or comparable worth) programmes. As Brown (1992: 10) suggests, they often involve 'extraordinary new levels of rationalization of the workplace: the techniques and instruments of job measurement, classification and job description required for its implementation make Taylorism look like child's play' (see also Lewis, 1988). When feminists work through some of the concrete consequences of political discourse, the manner in which Habermas has reconstructed the public sphere along the lines of universal masculinity becomes painfully apparent.

Feminism continues to grapple with the tensions between concrete and abstract, between particular and universal, in a way in which Habermas has not. Each side of these dualisms has formed different bases for claims-making in the history of feminism as a social movement – universalism manifests in the trajectory from suffrage to contemporary liberal feminism which stress the extension of general 'rights' to women, while another trajectory from early maternal feminism to 'cultural' feminism claims a unique and particular subject-position for women. While the former has been assailed for its uncritical acceptance of bourgeois individualism, the latter has been criticized for falsely universalizing 'female' to the exclusion of other axes of subject-formation such as class, race, ethnicity and sexual orientation.

Felski (1989a: 67–8) correctly recognizes that where feminism goes beyond liberal individualism is in its crucial dimension of communal solidarity: 'Feminism is defined by a fundamental tension and interaction between individual and collective identity.' Thus, feminism can 'engage in more diversified forms of discursive argumentation and critique which can take into account previously repressed aspects of personal and social life – emotion, desire, the body, personal relations – and which can remain receptive to the specificity of female experience and the need for cultural and group identity' (p. 71). Feminism as a social movement speaks *from* women's experience to issues which transcend the *particular* aspects of that experience – issues such as poverty, environmental destruction, violence, war, racism. At the same time, we do not lose sight of the particular aspects – that it is no mere coincidence that, for example, poverty and violence are disproportionately experienced by women, and by some women more than others. It is the willingness of recent feminist theory to grapple with the tension between the particular and universal, between the concrete and abstract, between the centred and decentred conceptions of the subject, that contains the potential for theorizing resistive agency, on the part of both collective and individual subjects. Felski, writing from the perspective of literary criticism, finds in Habermas the potential for overcoming a problem which he himself has not elaborated — a way of confronting the tension between particular and universal. She uses his concept of a communicatively rational public sphere to articulate a feminist counter-public which transcends the oppositions of essentialism/nominalism and materialism/idealism which have plagued feminist theory. In her framework, a feminist counter-public 'does not claim a represent-ative universality but demarcates a gender-specific space' and at the same time directs its discourse *outwards*, 'challenging existing structures of authority through political activity and theoretical critique' (1989a: 233–4). This simultaneous constitution of a space for inward-looking collective identity-formation and for outer-directed opposition embodies the tension between particularity and universality. Furthermore, it recognizes the problematic construc-tion of gendered interests, which are continually cross-cut by other oppositional interests, such as race, class and sexual orientation. A feminist counter-public in these terms both affirms and critiques 'feminine' identity, and manifests itself, not as an autonomous institutional realm, but as 'a series of political and cultural strategies which can be effective across a range of levels' (p. 235). As Felski summarizes its promise: 'The logic of a feminist counter-public sphere must thus be understood as ultimately *rational* in a Habermasian sense; that is, not in terms of an appeal to a transcendental substantive idea of reason, but in the procedural sense of engendering processes of argumentation and critique which contest existing norms and values and raise alternative validity claims' (p. 238).

The relationship of women to the state and political discourse remains complex and a number of interesting questions emerge out of this complexity. These include exploration of the different arenas in modern societies in which both individual and collective identities are formed, the degree to which 'public' spaces can engender resistance, and the necessity of critically examining the manner in which claims for 'citizenship', 'rights' and 'equality' are pressed in modern welfare states. As some of the literature I have reviewed suggests, the role of feminist discursive communities, as 'counter-publics', is crucial to the ongoing re-examination of such concepts as community, resistance and identity. This directs feminist theory to retain an awareness of the political nature of identity formation as both an individual and a collective project, and as one which, if it is to engender meaningful agency on the part of the subject, must be undertaken with full awareness of our 'historical memory', of 'what it cost us to get where we are' (Braidotti, 1991a: 165). A revitalized sense of public life must not be premised on the erasure of difference, but on its revaluation as the grounds for new forms of solidarity.

6

Feminist Theory as Critical Theory

In this final chapter, I want to review the ambivalent relationship of women to modernity, and of feminist theory to the debates around modernity and postmodernity. I will argue that there are both theoretical and political consequences related to the invisibility of women in the debates around modernity. Theoretically, we risk a slide into an unchecked postmodern pluralism, where feminism becomes but one voice among many. Politically, the interpretation of modernity has mapped out much of the terrain for current debates between right and left, within right and left, and between feminism and anti-feminism. Thus, I want to outline, as a point of departure, some of the issues which must lead off any attempt to advance the project of a feminist critical theory. Such a project cannot be undertaken by simply choosing to cast one's lot with modernity over postmodernity (or vice versa). It must begin by accepting — and empowering — concrete difference against abstract universals, but must do so in a way which preserves the opportunity for solidarity. As Braidotti (1991a: 164) has cautioned, unless we take the possibilities opened by difference as our starting point, women, 'the eternal servants at the banquets of life. . .will have to satisfy themselves with the crumbs of modernity'.

6.1 The Failure of the Classical Project

From the origins of classical sociological theory, the social differentiation of modern society has provided the underpinning of the discipline. If humans are defined as social beings, derived from aspects of their social existence, then there is a 'fluidity to the distribution of actors between the branches of the social division of labour' (Yeatman, 1986: 161). Given this fluidity, we understand the possibility for individuals to possess a 'role set' — to occupy different roles in different contexts of spaces and times, creating the possibility of an internally differentiated and complex individual personality. Yet social theory has not realized the promise in this for the theorization of personal life. Seeking to derive the individual solely from the social, 'the classical sociological project is caught by the inversion it has effected of the classical liberal starting point. In deprivatising the individual, it abolishes the field of social interaction that makes an individual a particular or unique individual' (p. 164). Domesticity, and hence women, are consigned to the 'natural', the 'pre-social', the 'primary group' or the 'embryo of community'. The implications are that two specialized types of personality are created — the masculine and the feminine — each with a particular set of social skills and orientations. By conflating the gender division of labour with the public/private division, we preclude the possibility that 'the differentiation and mutual dependence of public and domestic aspects of society' could be expressed 'within the same personality, and not as two distinct types of personality' (p. 171). From a feminist perspective, the failure of theories of modernity has been not to come to grips with difference adequately. The problem of order in the transition from traditional to modern societies was effectively solved in liberalism by the contract, and in sociology, by subverting the individual to the social. In taking the social as primary, the particular aspects of individuality were of waning interest, being consigned to questions of individual psychology, or 'nature'. The public/private dualism thus becomes expressed as the dualisms of universal/particular, rationality/emotionality, instrumental/expressive, formal/informal, political/apolitical, economic/familial — expressed by way of the division of labour which is expressed via the distinct personality types of masculine/feminine. As Benhabib (1987: 86) notes, the dehistoricization of the private sphere 'signifies that, as the male ego celebrates his passage from nature to culture. . .women remain in a timeless universe, condemned to repeat the cycles of life'. This is the theoretical trick by which women's subjectivity has been construed as being of a fundamentally different order than men's, and which sets up a gender polarity running through all levels, from psyche to polity. More accurately, we need to conceive of social relations, which exist in relationships of unequal power, as both inherited and re-created through their subjective inhabitation.

An analysis of feminist political struggles around citizenship and equality underscores the ambivalent relationship of feminism to modernity. Felski (1989c: 50) notes feminism's 'distinct engagement with the institutions and ideas of modernity', suggesting that it is 'in the contradictory spaces of such quintessentially modern institutions as bureaucracies and universities that feminism has made important relative gains in recent history through processes of educational and legal reform'. As a political movement, feminism continues to use egalitarian rhetoric as the basis of most of its political demands. Thus, feminism is wedded to the modern by virtue of its rootedness in the space opened up by rights discourse and by the ideals of the bourgeois public, but at the same time, its commitment to difference and diversity and its sceptical stance towards Reason call forth the postmodern. The relationship of women to modernity, and to social theory as a modern project, is truly one riven with contradictions and ambiguities. Feminism, I believe, constitutes both a critique of *and* a defence of modernity, so has a great stake in the modernity–postmodernity debates, which are at heart about the possibility of a 'subject' for social theory. A feminist analysis must recognize and build upon the insight that it can fully embrace neither an unreconstructed modernism's 'subject' nor postmodernism's rejection of the subject, by virtue of the fact that women as subjects have never been accorded the coherence, autonomy, rationality or agency of the subject which undergirds an unreconstructed modernism, and which postmodernism has deconstructed out of existence.

In a project which I find very sympathetic to my own, Stephen Leonard (1990: 37–8) suggests how we might, in the same way in which critical theory 'used Marx to move beyond Marx', use the insights of critical theory to 'move beyond the current impasse of modernist critical theory'. This impasse, he argues, is rooted in the lack of an 'addressee'. Leonard is not the first to note this problem in critical theory – the 'anonymity' of critical theory has become almost a standard criticism, particularly where Habermas's work is concerned (see, for example, Bernstein, 1976; Held, 1980; Livesay, 1985). This is crucial as well to his inability to overcome the opposition of universal and particular in the theory of communicative action. As Arafeh (1992: 27) notes: 'Habermas's preference for explicating *ideal* situations rather than *real* ones results in lip-service being given to the notion of a plural subject and the broader ramifications of such a position.' To begin to address this problem, and to locate the missing practical dimension, Leonard (1990: 46) suggests that critical theory must 'break from the "universalist" assumptions which have plagued attempts to realize "critical reason" since, perhaps, the Enlightenment'. It must give way to a 'plurality of critical theories'. It is not enough, however, to reassert the importance of the plural: 'the historical and contextual specificity of such theories cannot give up the claim to "reason" if they are to avoid being cast as merely arbitrary assertions of particularistic interests' (p. 53). Feminism, he suggests, is such a critical theory in action, in that it 'embodies a commitment to both solidarity and plurality' (p. 212) and is concerned less with the theoretical elaboration of emancipatory practice than it is with the 'practical demands that theory must meet' (p. 213). Leonard's analysis of feminist theory, while incomplete,[1] is a useful point of departure for considering how feminist theory can point the way past some of the theoretical and political roadblocks encountered by critical theory. As Braidotti (1991: 164) suggests, 'feminism is critical theory in that it reconnects the theoretical to the person – the question of identity – and both to the collective – the question of community; and it brings all of them to bear on the issue of entitlement'.

6.2 Agendas for Theory

Throughout this work I have attempted to juxtapose the considerable insights of structuralist formulations of the reproduction of capitalist patriarchy with more fluid conceptions of subjectivity and agency. As Barrett (1988a: x) suggests, a flexible vocabulary is necessary if we are to escape the tendency 'to assign rank in what is effectively a zero-sum game of structural determinism'. It is also suggests a necessary turn to developing theory from the standpoint of people, rather than that of structures or systems. It is only people who have needs, who act, who 'cause'. This does not mean that social structures are simply aggregates of individuals, for clearly there are relationships and patterns which are organized so as to go beyond the experience of any one individual. It is essential, however, to retain an awareness of these as historically constructed, originating in human agency — and not just agency conceived of as members of the dominant group unproblematically imposing their collective will. I have attempted to show, especially in chapters 2 and 5, that both men and women were (and are) active participants in the processes of historical construction. As Lerner (1986: 36) suggests: 'Once we abandon the concept of women as historical victims, acted upon by violent men, inexplicable "forces", and societal institutions, we must explain the central puzzle — women's participation in the construction of the system that subordinates her.' If we dispense with the notion of some single unitary interest (capital accumulation, patriarchal domination) which provides 'the' logic of oppression, then there is room for recovery of the concept of 'unintended consequences'. As Hall (1988: 45) suggests, interests 'are not only given as an objective feature of a structure of positions in a social system to which we are ascribed (and from which dangle the appropriate forms of consciousness) but they change historically'. That is, that given certain historical conditions, women make what may be very reasonable choices (or perhaps the only 'rational' choice available), the long-run consequences of which are to create and re-create the conditions for their subordination. Specific practices may mean very different things depending on whether we take the point of view of the individual or the point of view of the 'system'.

Gordon (1986: 23) notes that the contradiction between domination and resistance in studying women's history has its parallel in the structure versus agency debate in Marxism. 'This debate unfortunately has often been reduced to a schema in which structural analysis implies determination, while analysis in terms of human agency implies indeterminacy or contingency. . . .Usually it is the dominant groups who can have individual agency, while the subordinated appear locked in "structures".' Bryan Turner (1987: 195) suggests that 'sociology needs to develop a perspective on resistance and resignation as the counterpart to the overriding emphasis on control and management'. While I fully sympathize with his project, rather than seeing the theorization of resistance and resignation as a *counterpart* to the theorization of control and management, I would suggest that they are in fact part of the same project. That is, resistance occurs only within parameters of control, and resignation within management, and vice versa. One cannot conceive of one without the other. Turner suggests a threefold conceptualization of an 'ontology of human resistance': enselfment, embodiment and empowerment. By enselfment, he refers to 'the capacity for consciousness of one's particularity' (p. 195). This has some resonance with Giddens's notion of 'self-monitoring' or self-reflexive behaviour on the part of actors as fundamental to the theorization of the relationship between individual and society. The notion of embodiment rejects the Cartesian mind/body split, and emphasizes that 'our actions are the actions of embodied agency rather than a socialized will (p. 197). Finally, the dimension of empowerment implies a 'capacity for action on the part of knowledgeable, embodied agents capable of conscious experience and effectivity in the everyday world'. Turner conceptualizes these dimensions of the agent as parallel to certain structural dimensions of society: enselfment as corresponding to the ideological, embodiment as corresponding to the economic, and empowerment as corresponding to the political. It is in setting up these correspondences that Turner exposes his masculinist bias, for only male bodies and the male experience of embodiment can be so neatly separated from ideological and political discourses. In locating the body as a site of resistance, Turner suggests that bodily needs require engagement with pre-existing social relations and social structures mediated by consumptive practices, creating a certain dependency, yet 'we clearly enjoy a certain sovereignty and spontaneity over our phenomenal embodiment' (p. 199). It is historically women's *lack* of sovereignty over their bodies, that is, the ideological and political, not just economic, control of their bodies, which has grounded, and continues to ground, their experience of embodiment in a way that is fundamentally different from that of the male. With Turner, I would agree that embodiment is a crucial component of an ontology of resistance, but against him, I would argue that embodiment must be construed as gendered — a dimension which he neglects to recognize, and one which has profound consequences for his theorization of enselfment and empowerment.

West (1988b) has developed a framework for the analysis of Afro-American oppression which I think is paradigmatic for feminism. He employs what he terms a 'neo-Gramscian' approach which rejects the discursive reductionism and antitotalism of poststructuralism, but welcomes efforts 'to dismantle the logocentric and a priori aspects of the Marxist tradition':

> In other words, I accent the *demystifying* moment in their genealogical and deconstructive practices which attack hegemonic Western discourses that invoke universality, scientificity, and objectivity in order to hide cultural plurality, conceal the power-laden play of differences and preserve hierarchical class, gender, racial, and sexual orientational relations (p. 18).

West's framework has three 'moments': genealogical inquiry into hegemonic logics (or 'discourses') and their counterhegemonic possibilities; microinstitutional (or localized) analyses of 'the mechanisms that inscribe and sustain these logics' in everyday life and their counterhegemonic possibilities; and a macrostructural analysis of 'modes of overdetermined class exploitation and political repression' and their counterhegemonic possibilities (pp. 21–2). The first 'moment', genealogical inquiry, might include explorations of the discourses of religion, science and the Western philosophy of identity which have historically constructed sexual difference as hierarchy. In particular, scientific discourses (for example, on scientific management, scientific child-rearing, sociobiology) have acted as the great legitimators of hierarchy and oppression. The second 'moment', that of localized, microinstitutional analysis, takes 'the everyday world as problematic' (D. Smith, 1987), exploring the specific, historically bounded playing out of these hegemonic logics in the work-place, the family, the marketplace, and so on. The third 'moment', macrostructural analysis, ensures that we do not retreat behind the insights of Marx, but radically build upon them. It is a neo-Gramscian framework in that it uses Gramsci's metaphor of a 'historic bloc' to replace the traditional Marxian base–superstructure metaphor, and thus promotes a 'radically historical approach in which the economic, political, cultural and ideological regions of a social formation are articulated and elaborated in the form of overdetermined and often contradictory class and nonclass processes' (West, 1988b: 20–1). This allows us to grasp that there *are* historical structural constraints on agency, but as West stresses: 'Given the historical process, many structural constraints can become conjunctural opportunities' (p. 24). Herein lies the potential for identifying counterhegemonic possibilities – in a word, resistance. Counterhegemonic possibilities, as West suggests, must be identified at each level – from the emergence of emancipatory discourses, through localized resistance in the work-place to the more traditional Marxist focus on 'objective' economic crisis.

How might this analytic framework inform feminist theory? As I have tried to demonstrate throughout this work, no one level of analysis (psychoanalytic, economic, cultural, political) adequately captures the degree to which gender is woven into social life, yet neither can any level of analysis be jettisoned or collapsed into another. With a framework such as the one West has outlined, we can have our political economy and our discourse theory too, using the insights of each to illuminate the silences of the other. It also suggests a necessary break with any logocentric theory as the blueprint for practice. As Aronowitz and Giroux (1985: 116) stress:

[T]he basis for generating a new critical and radical theory appropriate to the problems and lived experiences of the twentieth century demands a new discourse, one that is informed by the legacy of a critical Marxism but that, in the final analysis, has to break with its most fundamental assumptions and, as such, break with Marxism as the master discourse of any emancipatory project.

Where Juliet Mitchell could suggest in 1971 that we needed to ask feminist questions and come up with Marxist answers, we can now ask feminist questions and come up with *feminist* answers. To do so, however, inevitably raises questions of the foundations of such a project. Contemporary feminist theory has not been immune to the epistemological upheavals which have characterized the social sciences and humanities in the last few decades. As Felski (1989c: 35) poses the question: 'How, then, is feminism to legitimate and sustain its own critique of patriarchy, once it recognizes the existence of a more general legitimation crisis which questions the grounding and authority of all forms of knowledge?'.

A considerable body of literature on feminist methodologies has emerged, with a variety of ways of classifying feminist methodologies and their underlying epistemological assumptions. Sandra Harding (1986) and Mary Hawkesworth (1989), in reviewing this literature, agree on three key epistemological strains in feminism: feminist empiricism, feminist standpoint theories, and feminist postmodernism.

Feminist empiricism aims its critique at eliminating sexism as a bias which violates the goal of objectivity which is central to the pursuit of scientific knowledge. Thus, sociologist Margrit Eichler (1988) suggests that the ultimate goal of feminist research is the development of a non-sexist approach in the social sciences, to make our knowledge of the social world more complete. She advocates a modified notion of objectivity — stripped of its association with political detachment and value-freedom — as an 'asymptotically approachable but unreachable goal, with the elimination of sexism in research as a station along the way' (p. 14). Similarly, political theorist Judith Evans (1986) has argued that the methods and techniques of political theory are essentially value-free, but it is 'the assumptions of the investigator and the way they influence the use of technique that are biased' (p. 4). Feminist empiricism, then, accepts the search for objective knowledge as an overriding goal, and sees the removal of masculine biases as essential to working towards this goal — as necessary for the production of more objective, better knowledge. For example, much of the literature on gender, work and class, which I reviewed in chapter 2, is rooted in a feminist empiricist standpoint, with the key arguments revolving around how better to define class to account for the experience of both men and women.

Feminist standpoint theories are more critical of the 'scientific method' and its search for objective knowledge, charging that it is irreversibly flawed by its androcentrism. They suggest a 'successor science' which is distinctly feminist, privileging the standpoint of women in a way which claims 'to overcome the dichotomizing that is characteristic of the Enlightenment/bourgeois world view and its science' (Harding, 1986: 142). Dorothy Smith (1987) and Nancy Hartsock (1985, 1987) are representative of this epistemological strand, which expresses a distinct hermeneutical component. Both Smith's 'sociology for women'[2] and Hartsock's 'feminist standpoint' suggest that the social position of women allows them, as did the position of the proletariat for Marx, a privileged, more complete, and less distorted view of the world than that available to the dominant group. Hartsock extends this to argue that knowledge gained from a selfconsciously marginal position does not aspire to be totalizing: 'marginalized groups are far less likely to mistake themselves for the universal "man" ' (Hartsock, 1987: 205).

Both Harding and Hawkesworth suggest that feminist standpoint theories anticipate feminist postmodernism, in that once the premise of a distinct feminist standpoint from which to comprehend the world is accepted, it is only a small leap to accept that there are a myriad of positions and knowledges, none of which can be privileged. For feminist postmodernism, it is only a decisive break with the legacy of the Enlightenment – an abandonment of the search for any certain foundation for knowledge – that can allow this plurality of understandings. Yet this belies the very real political interests which underlie feminist theory, which are necessarily founded on a belief that a feminist perspective is superior to a non-feminist perspective. This impasse leads Harding to argue for a deliberate epistemological instability, an embracing of the incoherencies of these various positions, as 'we do not know and should not know just what we want to say about a number of conceptual choices with which we are presented – except that the choices themselves create no-win dilemmas for our feminisms' (1986: 244). Hawkesworth, on the other hand, suggests that epistemological debates should be shifted from the status of 'the knower', to claims about 'the known'. That is, rather than interrogating the subjectivity of the investigator as grounds for a feminist critique, we are directed instead to investigate 'the adequacy of the standards of evidence, criteria of relevance, modes of analysis, and strategies of argumentation privileged by the dominant traditions' (Hawkesworth, 1989: 551). Shifting the focus to the adequacy of 'the known' requires a 'minimalist standard of rationality that requires that belief be apportioned to evidence and that no assertion be immune from critical assessment' (p. 556). While this is a helpful direction to chart for a critical feminist epistemology, it requires elaboration of just what standards are to be used to measure the strength of rational argument and by what means we can detect distortions of 'fact'. To do so places some responsibility back on the 'knower'.

I believe that we can frame a critical feminist epistemology, in a way which avoids the either/or choices associated with most classification schemes, but which requires the knower to situate herself, by beginning with the typology of 'knowledge-interests' posited by Habermas (1968/1971), in which all knowledge-seeking activity is inherently connected to interests. Empirical-analytical knowledge has an interest in control and prediction. Knowledge so gained may be judged only as to its correctness according to rational-purposive criteria. Hermeneutic-historical knowledge has an interest in understanding and may be judged according to its adequacy of meaning. These first two knowledge-interests can only address the question of 'what is'. Critical-emancipatory knowledge asks not only 'what is', but 'what ought to be'. It is directed towards the transformation of oppressive realities and may be judged as to its success in enlightening its participants.[3] Feminism as a politically motivated enterprise is necessarily concerned with critical-emancipatory knowledge. As Morrow (1985: 713) stresses, Habermas's distinction between these three types of knowledge-interests 'does not seek to question the possibility and the potential of the first two forms of knowledge, but does demand that they situate their self-understanding in relation to each other as well as the normative critique of domination'. As Habermas (1968/1971: 310) insists, a critical social science must go beyond the production of nomological knowledge 'to determine when theoretical statements grasp invariant regularities of social action as such, and when they express ideologically frozen relations of dependence that can in principle be transformed'. This is, of course, the essence of the feminist project.

The postmodern project is most problematic when it comes to recognizing the *interested* nature of feminism. In the social sciences, Steven Seidman (1991, 1992) has emerged as one of the most vocal proponents of a postmodern turn in social theory. In doing so, and in a manner typical of those who advocate this turn, Seidman paints a particularly wooden picture of 'modernists', uses feminist critiques of science as 'evidence' for the need to be postmodern, and presents them in such a way as to suggest that feminism is inevitably a postmodern position. He argues that postmodernism is the best course for the social sciences because it (presumably subsuming feminism) has *uniquely* challenged 'the modernist notion that science itself. . .is a privileged form of reason' (Seidman and Wagner, 1992: 4). He moves easily from the recognition that feminists have 'analyzed critically the politics of science in its normative constructions of femininity and womanhood' (1991: 134) to the assertion that it is *postmodernists* that have exposed science as 'a social force enmeshed in particular cultural and power struggles' (p. 134-5). He advocates an anti-foundationalist stance, arguing that there can be no secure analytic foundations for social scientific knowledge, yet at the same time suggests that we should conceive of social theory as 'narrative with moral intent' (1992). What is unclear is how one can sustain any practical and moral intent while simultaneously eschewing such 'core modernist concepts' as 'progress, domination, liberation and humanity' (1991: 144). How for example, could we unequivocally defend reproductive freedom for women, without some minimal conception of humanity which includes bodily integrity? While I am in broad agreement with much of Seidman's indictment of positivist hegemony in the sociological tradition, and with his call for a more contextualized, pragmatic form of theorizing, I believe that feminist theorizing cannot evade the question of the normative foundations of theory, and the necessity of the 'minimal criteria of validity' Benhabib (1990: 125).

The elaboration of a normative foundation for critical feminist theory remains to be undertaken. Clearly such a project cannot be built, as in classical Marxism, on the foundation of a coherent subject who must only come to complete consciousness to understand what must be done. The shift required is, in Habermas's vocabulary, one from a 'paradigm of consciousness' to a 'paradigm of mutual understanding' – from subject-centred reason to communicative reason (Habermas, 1985/1987b: 310). Such a shift, however, must be premised on a less transcendental version of discourse than Habermas's 'universal pragmatics', whose untenable universalism undermines its critical potential. As Leonard (1990: 256) suggests, Habermas's quest for new universals risks precluding 'from "rational" discourse a consideration of the historically contingent and contextually specific self-understandings (and emancipatory ideals) of the same social movements he purports to endorse'. The 'normative scepticism' of postmodernism, however, does not provide an alternative, as it leaves us without room for 'taking up solidarity with those who are oppressed' (p. 258).

As Felski has argued, feminist struggles have always been characterized by a 'fundamental tension and interaction between individual and collective identity' (1989a: 67–8). This permits us to analyse feminism, as Felski has done, as engaging in forms of argumentation and critique which are receptive to both the specificity of female experience and the need for cultural and group identity. As I argued in chapter 5, feminism as a social movement speaks *from* women's experience to address issues which transcend the *particular* aspects of that experience. It is the willingness of recent feminist theory to grapple with the tension between the particular and universal, between the concrete and abstract, between the centred and decentred conceptions of the subject, which gives it the potential to breathe new life into social theory. Feminist theory has always been critical of the manner in which the grand theories of modernity have reified cultural categories which structure gender in historically bounded, locally contingent ways, and, in agreement with some postmodern prescriptives, looks to the local and particular. Yet clearly some accounts of social life are more 'reasonable', by some minimal criteria, than others. Unless criteria which transcend the local are invoked, it is not possible to distinguish between progressive and regressive theories, or to claim, for example, that a feminist's account of gender inequality is superior to a sociobiologist's or a religious fundamentalist's account.

Feminism, at its best, is a project of redefinition of the relationship between the individual and society, seeking 'an integration of the individual and the collective in an ongoing process of authentic individualism and genuine connectedness' (Ferguson, 1984: 157). This entails recognition that 'any radical reconstruction of either private life or public life entails reconstruction of the relationship between them' (p. 201). The task for feminism, then, is to reject prevailing modes of interpretation and undertake the inherently normative project of creating alternative interpretations. In uncovering the suppressed history of women, we are only now reaching an understanding of how any mode of interpretation is the result of contestation and resistance, and how other possible modes have been suppressed.

The need to argue for a normative foundation for feminism has never been more urgent. As the opposition confidently points to Christian fundamentalism or *laissez-faire* conservatism, cloaked in terms of 'individual rights', as its justification, feminist theory has grappled with questions of choice. As Ehrenreich and English pointed out more than a decade ago: 'feminism seems to become ever more determined about its undeterminedness, more nervously defensive of "choice" for its own sake, less and less prone to pass judgement on the alternatives, or to ask how these became choices in the first place' (1978: 291). The genesis of these alternatives and 'choices' must be subjected more thoroughly to open and public argument, to expose the structural inequalities which limit some voices while favouring others. To do so takes us beyond the arguments about whether feminism is inherently modern or postmodern, to consider more fully the outcomes of the ambivalent relationship of feminists to conventional standards of 'progress'.

The position that I wish to advocate for feminism might be called a 'critical modernism'. It has much in common with work by some theorists who accept the label postmodern — for example Fraser and Nicholson (1990) and West (1988a). Like them, I endorse a theory which is post-positivist, critical of the hegemony of Western 'reason', listens to 'local stories', rethinks the notion of a coherent pre-existing 'subject' and rejects the universalizing impulse of 'grand narratives'. However, I believe that it is possible radically to challenge the principles of the 'project of modernity' as it has been construed in Western social theory, and to reshape its categories of analysis, without severing all ties to its emancipatory aspirations.[4] Albrecht Wellmer captures this ambiguity well in his metaphor of the shifting image: depending on the vantage point, one can see either 'the end of an historical project: the project of modernity, the project of the European Enlightenment' or 'the contours of a radicalised modernism, or a self-enlightened enlightenment' (1985: 337).

A critical modernism must begin by problematizing the grand

narrative of modernity. Engendering modernity reveals that gender is not absent from the discourse of modernity – it was there all along but was not recognized, it has remained largely 'unthought'. But silence constitutes a special type of treatment – a strategic absence, or presence by absence. We need to historicize some of our basic concepts (such as the public/private distinction) to undermine some of the reified abstractions which have excluded women from analysis, to correct the one-sided story which misinforms social theory's self-understanding.

The overriding aim of this book has been the retrieval of women's experience, in all its diversity, from the margins of theory, to reposition it at the centre of the debates about modernity. This has not been undertaken, however, with an eye to replacing one account of modernity with another – albeit more gender-balanced – one. As Raymond Williams notes: 'the more we know of a particular form, practice, institution or period the less likely we are to be satisfied with any general analysis of it, however close' (1981: 181). Williams's comment is particularly apt given the explosion of feminist scholarship over the last few decades which suggests a turn to a more open, historically specific approach to the production and reproduction of women's subordination. I have stressed the historical creation of the gendered division of labour, and the fundamental part that gender plays in organizing, not just allocating, labour in our society. In the critique of theoretical explanations for the gendered division of labour, and particularly in the gender, work and class debates, I noted a failure to recognize that class is always expressed in gendered terms, resulting from a persistent reification of the public/private dualism and its coincidence with the gendered division of labour. I have emphasized the need to historicize, to make gender visible, the dualistic categories which underlie theories of modernity – public/private, individual/ society, family/economy. Once historicized in this fashion, they appear not as ossified structures, but as shifting and fluid mechanisms of regulating identities – to make legitimate the public expression of some identities, but to exclude others. I have also suggested that we need to take up the question of the subject, and in particular, gendered subjects, as a crucial level of analysis. The simultaneously individual and social nature of the subject, alluded to but never fully explored by Marx, sets the basis for a conception of gendered subjects who actively interpret, within historically available modes of interpretation, their identities. This interpretation involves negotiating the multiple and often contradictory components of subjectivity, and sets the stage whereby identity may become a political point of departure. Extending the analysis to the politics of regulating gender polarity provides the context for the interpretation of identities. An examination of the realm of political discourse on gender and its regulation reveals that neither one unitary interest (class, race, gender) nor one single agent of regulation unilaterally imposes its 'reproductive will'. I have suggested that feminist practice – or any critical practice – must be directed at a refashioning of the public sphere, exposing the limits of institutional reform premised upon universalistic notions of rights and justice which mask the underlying gender polarity. Finally, I have argued that our theoretical practice must be more selfconsciously critical, asking questions about how and why we seek the knowledge that we do.

I will conclude, then, with a call for a new theoretical eclecticism;[5] one which vigorously engages both the defenders and critics of the project of modernity, to ensure that women are not written out of yet another important theoretical turn. The issues raised by the postmodern critique are crucial – but far from signalling an end to theory, they underscore the importance of its revitalization. From a feminist perspective, modernity is a less finished project than even its staunchest defenders are willing to admit.

Notes

Introduction

1 In his chapter on 'Traditional and Critical Theory' Horkheimer (1972) provides a classic statement of critical theory as the emancipatory heir of the Enlightenment. Antonio (1989, 1990), Kellner (1989) and Leonard (1990) define critical theory as more closely tied to the Marxist tradition.

2 Useful sources for those seeking a more detailed analysis of some of these developments within feminist theory include Barrett and Phillips (1992), Braidotti (1991b), Brennan (1989), Butler and Scott (1992), Ferguson (1993), Fuss (1989), Hennessy (1993) and Nicholson (1990).

Chapter 1 Gender and Modernity: Classical Issues, Contemporary Debates

1 See, for example, Abercrombie, Hill and Turner (1986), Berman (1988), Kellner (1989), Rundell (1987), Sayer (1991), Smart (1990) and Turner (1990b).

2 Exceptions include Bologh (1990), Gane (1983), Kandal (1988), Nicholson (1986), Roth (1989–90), Sydie (1987), Thomas (1985), van Vucht Tijssen (1990) and Yeatman (1986). While not a detailed treatment, Sayer (1991) is noteworthy for his recognition of the gendered character of modernity and the neglect of this in the classical tradition.

3   See Donzelot (1980) and Lasch (1979) for similar themes. The basic argument rests on a relatively uncritical acceptance of the Oedipal model of ego development. Benjamin (1988) provides an insightful critique of the 'gender polarity' — the binary opposition of male and female — that grounds this model. I have adopted the term 'gender polarity', which is central to the analysis in chapter 4, from her work.

4   As Sayer (1991: 144) suggests, a more accurate metaphor might be the 'shell (*Gehäuse*) on a snail's back: a burden perhaps, but something impossible to live without, in either sense of the word. A cage remains an external restraint: unlock the door and one walks free. This *Gehäuse* is a prison altogether stronger, the armour of modern subjectivity itself. Dependency on "mechanized petrification" has become an integral part of who we are.'

5   The terminology here is problematic. In some usages, 'postmodernism' is taken to be synonymous with 'poststructuralism', in others it is synonymous with anything critical of mainstream culture. I will use the term 'postmodernist' to refer to a theoretical stance which identifies the current age as a unique era (literally 'post-' modern) and which rejects the possibility or desirability of resuscitating the Enlightenment project, and hence of normatively grounding an emancipatory practice, seeing these aspirations as both historically passé and inevitably oppressive. I will use the term 'poststructuralist' to refer to theories grounded in a refusal of the coherent theoretical subject and which emphasize the crucial role of language in representations of subjectivity and truth. Agger (1991) provides a useful discussion of these distinctions, suggesting, as I do here, that poststructuralism is primarily a theory of knowledge and language, while postmodernism is a theory of society, culture and history. The extent to which theorists have made these distinctions converge and overlap varies.

6   This is also the point of departure for Giddens's now classic treatise on Marx, Durkheim and Weber (1971) as the central core of social theory, which begins with the basic contention that 'the overwhelming interest of each of these authors was in the delineation of the characteristic structure of modern "capitalism" as contrasted with prior forms of society' (p. xvi).

Chapter 2   Rethinking the Gendered Division of Labour

1   Notable exceptions are Kanter (1977) on manager's wives, and Fowlkes (1980) on two person careers in medicine and academia.

2   'Caring' labour tends to be women's work when it is waged work as well – witness the vast majority of paid child-care, health and social service-workers who are women.

3   Bradley (1989: 24–26) uses a similar three-fold typology of explanatory theories, referring to them as the 'reproduction orientation', the 'production orientation' and the 'joint orientation'.

4   This is, of course, the case only for white women. Women of colour have never been granted the luxury of a 'feminine temperament', and have always been expected to perform heavy physical labour.

5   See, for example, Pahl (1984) and Redclift and Mingione (1985) on the growing significance of household economies against the background of economic restructuring.

Chapter 3   Social Reproduction and Socialist Feminist Theory

1   Useful sources for tracing this fragmentation include Anderson (1980), Antonio (1990), Aronowitz (1981, 2/1990), Kellner (1989) and Morrow (1991).

2   See Eagleton (1991: 148–158) for an excellent discussion of Althusser's conception of ideology as a 'breakthrough' in Marxism.

3   On Foucault's relationship to Marxism, see Poster (1984) and Smart (1983).

4   While the term 'French feminism' is often taken to be synonymous with the poststructuralist variety, see Jenson (1990) for a view of the broader range of French feminisms.

5   Bradley (1989), for example, prefers the term 'masculinist' to patriarchal.

Chapter 4   Gendered Identities

1   Jean Elshtain makes a somewhat similar critique of economistic Marxist–feminist theories of reproduction, charging that '. . .they see the family only as a unit defined by its role in the provision of domestic labour and the reproduction cycle of labour-power through which it relates to the functional prerequisites of capitalism. What of family loyalty? Intimacy? Responsibility? Cross-generational ties? Love? Hate?' (1981: 138).

However, I disagree sharply with Elshtain's conclusions on the direction that feminist theory should take to correct this narrow view of reproduction. Her position is based on an overly valorized conception of motherhood which replicates the dualism of feminine/nurturance versus masculine/autonomy, and calls for women to embrace the private world of mothering.

2 The term 'gender polarity' is from Jessica Benjamin (1988).

3 The difference between de Beauvoir's philosophical essentialism and Firestone's biological essentialism is best summarized by Firestone herself (1970: 7): 'Why postulate a fundamental Hegelian concept of otherness as the final explanation – and then carefully document the biological and historical circumstances that have pushed the class "woman" into such a category – when one has never seriously considered the much simpler and more likely possibility that this fundamental dualism sprang from the sexual division itself?'.

4 Rosaldo later modified her position somewhat in an article (1980) published shortly before her death.

5 Smith (1988: xxx) explains his use of the term: 'The word "cerning" conflates and plays simultaneously upon two rarely used English verbs – "to cern" and "to cerne". The first means to "accept and inheritance or a patrimony". . .[the second] means "to encircle" or "to enclose" '.

6 By way of analogy, Matthews (1984: 14) suggests that 'we can talk of an economic order as being the ordering of people's relationships to the means of production and consumption which exist in every society. Such an ordering has no essential nature, but may be variously feudal or capitalist or communist.'

7 The persistence of oppressive social relations and the apparent complicity of the oppressed in maintaining them is problematic in poststructuralist accounts, especially given their emphasis on the instability (rather than their tenacity) of social systems.

Chapter 5 Gender Politics: Regulation and Resistance

1 See Eisenstein (1988) for a more extended discussion of this point, with reference to struggles over reproductive rights in the United States.

2 To illustrate this, Abrams (1988) suggests we substitute the word 'god' for the word 'state', drawing an analogy to the study of religion: 'The task of the sociologist of religion is the explanation of religious practice (churches) and religious belief (theology): he [sic] is not called upon to debate, let alone to believe in, the existence of god' (p. 80).

3   We might apply Abrams's suggestion (see note 2 above) here as well, substituting 'god' for 'the family'.
4   During the American elections of 1992, the incumbent Republican Party made 'family values', narrowly interpreted as those which support the white, traditional, one-earner nuclear family, the centrepiece of their re-election campaign, which included a strong move to recriminalize and restrict abortion. While they were defeated, they were successful in defining political discourse around 'family values', forcing the victorious, and more liberal, Democratic Party to temper some of its proposed reforms, such as increased civil rights for gays and lesbians.
5   See, for example, the analyses in Fierlbeck (1991) and Turner (1990a).

Chapter 6   Feminist Theory as Critical Theory

1   One of the most glaring gaps in his treatment of feminist theory, given his overall project, is his relative neglect of feminist theory which has directly engaged with the critical theory tradition. He does not consider the work of Jessica Benjamin (1977, 1978, 1988) or Patricia Mills (1987) at all, and only treats briefly the innovative and important attempt by Nancy Fraser (1989) to develop a critical-feminist theory.
2   Smith's feminist standpoint theory was originally elaborated in the mid-1970s (see Smith, 1974) and was tremendously influential in my own discovery of Marxist-feminist theory as an undergraduate. It was through her work that I was first introduced to, and gained an interest in, a feminist sociology of knowledge. While my more recent interests have taken me in a somewhat different direction, my debt to her path-breaking work far exceeds the number of direct citations in this book.
3   As Habermas has argued, 'in the process of enlightenment, there are only participants' (1963/1973: 40).
4   Aronowitz and Giroux (1991) argue for a similar direction. They point out that modernism and postmodernism may each be deployed in either regressive or progressive ways, and conclude that choosing between the two is a less useful path than 'drawing on the best insights of each' (p. 59).
5   I use the term 'eclecticism' here in a very different sense from Hennessy (1993: 15), who uses it to characterize a mode of reading which 'uncritically links explanatory frames without making visible the contesting assumptions on which they are often premised'. On the

contrary, I think that it is only through a critical eclecticism that we can achieve what she calls 'ideology critique': 'a social analytic whose legitimacy is argued for not on the grounds of its scientific Truth but on the basis of its explanatory power and its commitment to emancipatory social change'.

References

Abbott, Patricia and Sapsford, Roger 1987: *Women and Social Class*. London and New York: Tavistock.

Abercrombie, N., Hill, S. and Turner, B. 1986: *Sovereign Individuals of Capitalism*. London, Sydney and Boston: Allen & Unwin.

Abrams, Philip 1988: Notes on the difficulty of studying the state (1977). *Journal of Historical Sociology*, 1 (1), 58–89.

Agger, Ben 1977: Dialectical sensibility I: theory, scientism and empiricism. *Canadian Journal of Social and Political Theory*, 1, 1–30.

——1991: Critical theory, poststructuralism, postmodernism: their sociological relevance. *Annual Review of Sociology*, 17, 105–31.

Alcoff, Linda 1988: Cultural feminism versus post-structuralism: the identity crisis in feminist theory. *Signs*, 13 (3), 405–36.

Alexander, Jeffrey 1987: The dialectic of individuation and domination: Weber's rationalization theory and beyond. In Sam Whimster and Scott Lash (eds), *Max Weber, Rationality and Modernity*, London, Sydney and Boston: Allen & Unwin, 185–206.

Alexander, Sally 1984: Women, class and sexual difference in the 1830's and 1840's: some reflections on the writing of a feminist history. *History Workshop Journal*, 17 (Spring), 125–49.

Althusser, Louis and Balibar, Etienne 1965/1970: *Reading 'Capital'*, trans. Ben Brewster. London: New Left Books [orig. pubd as *Lire le 'Capital'*, Paris: François Maspero].

Anderson, Karen 1987: A gendered world: women, men and the political economy of the seventeenth-century Huron. In Heather Jon Maroney and Meg Luxton (eds), *Feminism and Political Economy*, London and Toronto: Methuen, 121–38.

Anderson, Perry 1980: *Arguments within English Marxism*. London: Verso.

——1983: *In the Tracks of Historical Materialism*. London: Verso.

Antonio, Robert J. 1989: The normative foundations of emancipatory theory: evolutionary versus pragmatic perspectives. *American Journal of Sociology*, 94 (4), 721–48.

——1990: The decline of the grand narrative of emancipatory modernity: crisis or renewal in neo-Marxian theory. In George Ritzer (ed.), *Frontiers of Social Theory: The New Syntheses*, New York: Columbia University Press, 88–116.

Apple, Michael 1983: Introduction. In Philip Wexler, *Critical Social Psychology*, London and New York: Routledge & Kegan Paul.

Arafeh, Sousan 1992: The object of sociological inquiry: multiple subject positions, Habermas and post-modernism. Unpublished paper, presented to the Canadian Sociology and Anthropology Association Annual Meetings, University of Prince Edward Island, Charlottetown, Prince Edward Island, 1–4 June, 1992.

Arat-Koç, Sedef 2/1990: Importing housewives: non-citizen domestic workers and the crisis of the domestic sphere in Canada. In Sedef Arat-Koç, Meg Luxton and Harriet Rosenberg (eds), *Through the Kitchen Window: The Politics of Home and Family* (2nd enlarged edn), Toronto: Garamond, 81–103.

Armstrong, Pat 1984: *Labour Pains: Women's Work in Crisis*. Toronto: Women's Press.

Armstrong, Pat and Armstrong, Hugh 1983: Beyond sexless class and classless sex: towards feminist Marxism. *Studies in Political Economy*, 10 (Winter), 7–43.

——1984: More on Marxism and feminism: a response to Patricia Connelly. *Studies in Political Economy*, 15 (Fall), 179–84.

——1990: *Theorizing Women's Work*. Toronto: Garamond.

Aronowitz, Stanley 1988: The production of scientific knowledge: science, ideology and Marxism. In Cary Nelson and Lawrence Grossberg (eds), *Marxism and the Interpretation of Culture*, Chicago: University of Illinois Press, 519–41.

——1981/1990: *The Crisis in Historical Materialism* (2nd edn). Minneapolis: University of Minnesota Press.

Aronowitz, Stanley and Giroux, Henry 1985: *Education under Siege*. South Hadley, MA: Bergin & Garvey.

——1991: *Postmodern Education: Politics, Culture and Social Criticism*. Minneapolis: University of Minnesota Press.

Bakker, Isabella 1988: Women's employment in comparative perspective. In Jane Jenson, Elisabeth Hagen and Ceallaigh Reddy (eds), *Feminization of the Labour Force: Paradoxes and Promises*, Cambridge: Polity Press, 17–44.

Balbo, Laura 1987: Family, women and the state: notes toward a typology of family roles and public intervention. In Charles S. Maier (ed.), *Changing Boundaries of the Political*, Cambridge: Cambridge University Press, 201–19.

Banting, Keith 1987: The welfare state and inequality in the 1980s. *Canadian Review of Sociology and Anthropology*, 24 (3), 309–38.

Barnsley, Jan 1988: Feminist action, institutional reaction. *Resources for Feminist Research*, 17 (3), 18–21.

Barrett, Michele 1980: *Women's Oppression Today*. London: Verso.

——1984: Rethinking women's oppression: reply to Brenner and Ramas. *New Left Review*, 146, 123–8.

——1988a: Introduction. In Michèle Barrett, *Women's Oppression Today* (Rev. edn), London: Verso, v–xxxiv.

——1988b: Comment on a paper by Christine Delphy. In Cary Nelson and Lawrence Grossberg (eds), *Marxism and the Interpretation of Culture*, Chicago: University of Illinois Press, 268–9.

Barrett, Michele and MacIntosh, Mary 1982: *The Anti-Social Family*. London: Verso.

Barrett, Michele and Phillips, Anne (eds) 1992: *Destabilizing Theory*. Stanford, CA: Stanford University Press.

Baudrillard, Jean 1983: *In the Shadow of the Silent Majorities*. New York: Semiotext(e).

Beauvoir, Simone de 1949/1961: *The Second Sex*, trans. H.M. Parshley. New York: Bantam Books [orig. pubd as *Le deuxiène sexe*, Paris: Gallimard].

Beechey, Veronica 1987: *Unequal Work*. London: Verso.

Benhabib, Seyla 1986: *Critique, Norm and Utopia*. New York: Columbia University Press.

——1987: The generalized and the concrete other. In Seyla Benhabib and Drucilla Cornell (eds), *Feminism as Critique*, Oxford: Blackwell; Minneapolis: University of Minnesota Press, 77–95.

——1990: Epistemologies of postmodernism: a rejoinder to Jean-François Lyotard. In Linda Nicholson (ed.), *Feminism/Postmodernism*, London: Routledge, 107–30.

Benhabib, Seyla and Cornell, Drucilla 1987: Introduction: beyond the politics of gender. In Seyla Benhabib and Drucilla Cornell (eds), *Feminism as Critique*, Oxford: Blackwell; Minneapolis: University of Minnesota Press, 1–15.

Benjamin, Jessica 1977: The end of internalization: Adorno's social psychology. *Telos*, 32, 42–64.

——1978: Authority and the family revisited: or, a world without fathers? *New German Critique*, 13, 35–58.

——1988: *The Bonds of Love: Psychoanalysis, Feminism and the Problem of Domination*. New York: Pantheon.

Berger, Brigette and Berger, Peter 1983: *The War over the Family: Capturing the Middle Ground*. New York: Anchor Books.

Berk, Sarah F. 1985: *The Gender Factory*. New York: Plenum Press.

Berman, Marshall 1982: *All that is Solid Melts into Air: The Experience of Modernity*. New York: Simon & Schuster.

Bernstein, Basil 1977: *Class, Codes and Control*. London: Routledge & Kegan Paul.

Bernstein, Richard J. 1976: *The Restructuring of Social and Political Theory*. Philadelphia: University of Pennsylvania Press.

Bhavnani, Kum-Kum and Coulson, Margaret 1986: Transforming socialist–feminism: the challenge of racism. *Feminist Review*, 23, 81–92.

Bologh, Roslyn Wallach 1987: Marx, Weber and masculine theorizing. In Norbert Wiley (ed.), *The Marx-Weber Debates*. London and Newbury Park, CA: Sage, 145–68.

——1990: *Love or Greatness? Max Weber and Masculine Thinking*. London: Unwin Hyman.

Bottomore, Tom (ed.) 1963: *Karl Marx: Early Writings*. London: C.A. Watts.

Bourdieu, Pierre 1977: *Outline of a Theory of Practice*. Cambridge: Cambridge University Press.

Bowles, Samuel and Gintis, Herbert 1976: *Schooling in Capitalist America*. New York: Basic Books.

Bradbury, Bettina 1984: Women and wage labour in a period of transition: Montreal, 1861–1881. *Histoire Sociale/Social History*, 17, 115–31.

Bradley, Harriet 1989: *Men's Work, Women's Work*. Cambridge: Polity Press; Minneapolis: University of Minnesota Press.

Braidotti, Rosi 1991a: The subject in feminism. *Hypatia*, 6 (2), 155–72.

——1991b: *Patterns of Dissonance*. New York: Routledge.

Brennan, Theresa (ed.) 1989: *Between Feminism and Psychoanalysis*. New York: Routledge.

Brenner, Johanna and Ramas, Maria 1984: Rethinking women's oppression. *New Left Review*, 144, 33–71.

Brown, Jennifer S. H. 1980: *Strangers in Blood: Fur Trade Families in Indian Country*. Vancouver: University of British Columbia Press.

Brown, Wendy 1992: Finding the man in the state. *Feminist Studies*, 18 (1), 7–34.

Bryant, Christopher G. A. and Jary, David 1991: Introduction: coming to terms with Anthony Giddens. In Christopher G. A. Bryant and David Jary (eds), *Giddens' Theory of Structuration: A Critical Appreciation*, London: Routledge, 1–31.

Burstyn, Varda 1985: Masculine dominance and the state. In Varda Burstyn and Dorothy Smith, *Women, Class, Family and the State*, Toronto: Garamond, 45–89.

Burton, Clare 1985: *Subordination: Feminism and Social Theory*. London, Sydney and Boston: Allen & Unwin.

Butler, Judith 1990: *Gender Trouble: Gender and the Subversion of Identity*. London: Routledge.

Butler, Judith and Scott, Joan (eds) 1992: *Feminists Theorize the Political*. New York: Routledge.

Calhoun, Craig 1992: Introduction: Habermas and the public sphere. In Craig Calhoun (ed.), *Habermas and the Public Sphere*, Cambridge, MA: MIT Press, 1–48.

Campbell, Beatrix 1987: *The Iron Ladies: Why Do Women Vote Tory?* London: Virago.

Chodorow, Nancy 1978: *The Reproduction of Mothering: Psychoanalysis and the Sociology of Gender*. Berkeley: University of California Press.

Cixous, Hélène (with Catherine Clément) 1985: *The Newly Born Woman*. Minneapolis: University of Minnesota Press.

Clark, J., Modgil, C. and Modgil, F. (eds) 1990: *Anthony Giddens: Consensus and Controversy*. London: Falmer Press.

Cockburn, Cynthia 1985: *Machinery of Dominance: Women, Men and Technical Know-How*. London: Pluto Press.

Cohen, Ira 1989: *Structuration Theory and the Constitution of Social Life*. London: Macmillan.

Cohen, Jean L. and Arato, Andrew 1992: *Civil Society and Political Theory*. Cambridge, MA: MIT Press.

Cohen, Marjorie 1987: *Women's Work, Markets and Economic Development in Nineteenth Century Ontario*. Toronto: University of Toronto Press.

Connell, R. W. 1979: A critique of the Althusserian approach to class. *Theory and Society*, 8 (3), 321–45.

——1983: *Which Way is Up? Essays on Sex, Class and Culture*. London, Sydney and Boston: Allen & Unwin.

——1987: *Gender and Power*. Cambridge: Polity Press; Stanford, CA: Stanford University Press.

——1990: The state, gender and sexual politics: theory and appraisal. *Theory and Society*, 19, 507–44.

Connell, R. W., Ashenden, D. H., Kessler, S. and Dowsett, G. W. 1982: *Making the Difference: Schools, Families and Social Division*. London, Sydney and Boston: Allen & Unwin.

Connelly, Patricia 1983: On Marxism and feminism. *Studies in Political Economy*, 12 (Fall), 153–61.

Connelly, Patricia and MacDonald, Martha 1986: Women's work: domestic and wage labour in a Nova Scotia community. In Roberta Hamilton and Michèle Barrett (eds), *The Politics of Diversity*, London: Verso, 53–80.

Conrad, Shirley 1986: Sundays always make me think of home: time and place in Canadian women's history. In Veronica Strong-Boag and Anita Clair Fellman (eds), *Rethinking Canada: The Promise of Women's History*, Toronto: Copp Clark Pitman, 67–81.

Coontz, Stephanie 1988: *The Social Origins of Private Life: A History of American Families 1600–1900*. London: Verso.

Cornell, Drucilla and Thurschwell, Adam 1987: Femininity, negativity, intersubjectivity. In Seyla Benhabib and Drucilla Cornell (eds), *Feminism as Critique*, Minneapolis: University of Minnesota Press, 143–62.

Corrigan, Philip 1990: *Social Forms/Human Capacities: Essays in Authority and Difftrence*. London: Routledge.

Corrigan, Philip and Sayer, Derek 1985: *The Great Arch: English State Formation as Cultural Revolution*. Oxford: Blackwell.

Cowan, Ruth Schwartz 1983: *More Work for Mother*. New York: Basic Books.

Craib, Ian 1984: *Modern Social Theory*. London: Harvester Press.

——1992: *Anthony Giddens*. London: Routledge.

Craig, C., Garnsey, E. and Rubery, J. 1984: *Payment Structures and Smaller Firms: Women's Employment in Segmented Labour Markets*. Research Paper 48. London: Department of Employment.

——1985: Labour market segmentation and women's employment: a case study from the United Kingdom. *International Labour Review*, 124, 267–80.

Crompton, Rosemary and Sanderson, Kay 1990: *Gendered Jobs and Social Change*. London: Unwin Hyman.

Dalley, G. 1988: *Ideologies of Caring: Rethinking Community and Collectivism*. London: Macmillan.

Daly, Mary 1978: *Gyn/ecology: The Metaethics of Radical Feminism*. Boston: Beacon Press.

Davies, Marjorie 1982: *Women's Place is at the Typewriter: Office Work and Office Workers 1870–1930*. Philadelphia: Temple University Press.

de Lauretis, Teresa 1986: Feminist studies/critical studies: issues, terms and contexts. In Teresa de Lauretis (ed.), *Feminist Studies/Critical Studies*, Bloomington: Indiana University Press, 1–19.

Delphy, Christine 1984: *Close to Home*. London: Hutchinson.

Delphy, Christine and Leonard, Diana 1986: Class analysis, gender analysis and the family. In Rosemary Crompton and Michael Mann (eds), *Gender and Stratification*, Cambridge: Polity Press, 57–73.

Dex, Shirley 1985: *The Sexual Division of Work*. Brighton: Harvester Press.

Diamond, Irene and Quinby, Lee (eds) 1988: *Feminism and Foucault: Reflections on Resistance*. Boston: Northeastern University Press.

Diaz-Cotto, Juanita 1991: Women and crime in the United States. In Chandra Talpad Mohanty, Ann Russo and Lourdes Torres (eds), *Third World Women and the Politics of Feminism*, Bloomington: Indiana University Press, 197–211.

Dickinson, James and Russell, Bob 1986: Introduction: the structure of reproduction in capitalist society. In James Dickinson and Bob Russell (eds), *Family, Economy and State: The Reproduction Process under Capitalism*, Toronto: Garamond, 1–20.

Dinnerstein, Dorothy 1976: *The Mermaid and the Minotaur*. New York: Harper & Row.

Donovan, Josephine 1985: *Feminist Theory: The Intellectual Traditions of American Feminism*. New York: Frederick Ungar.

Donzelot, Jacques 1980: *The Policing of Families*. London: Hutchinson.

Durkheim, Emile 1893/1933: *Division of Labour in Society*, trans. W. D. Halls. New York: Macmillan [orig. pubd as *De la division du travail social*, Paris].

——1897/1951: *Suicide*, trans J. A. Spaulding and G. Simpson. New York: Free Press [orig. pubd as *Le suicide*, Paris].

Eagleton, Terry 1991: *Ideology*. London: Verso.

Edholm, Felicity, Harris, Olivia and Young, Kate 1977: Conceptualising women. *Critique of Anthropology*, 9/10, 101–30.

Edwards, Richard C. 1979: *Contested Terrain: The Transformation of the Workplace in the Twentieth Century*. New York: Basic Books.

Ehrenreich, Barbara and English, Deirdre 1978: *For their own Good: 150 Years of the Experts' Advice to Women*. New York: Doubleday.

Eichler, Margrit 1988: *Nonsexist Research Methods*. London: Unwin Hyman.

Eisenstein, Sarah 1983: *Give us Bread but Give us Roses*. London: Routledge & Kegan Paul.

Eisenstein, Zillah 1979: *Capitalist Patriarchy and the Case for Socialist Feminism*. New York: Monthly Review Press.

——1981: *The Radical Future of Liberal Feminism*. New York: Longman.

——1982: The sexual politics of the New Right: understanding the crisis of liberalism. In N. Keohane, M. Rosaldo and B. Gelpi (eds), *Feminist Theory: A Critique of Ideology*. Chicago: University of Chicago Press, 77–98.

——1984: *Feminism and Sexual Equality*. New York: Monthly Review Press.

——1988: *The Female Body and the Law*. Berkeley: University of California Press.

Elshtain, Jean B. 1981: *Public Man, Private Woman*. Princeton, NJ: Princeton University Press.

Engel, Stephanie 1980: Femininity as tragedy: re-examining the new narcissism. *Socialist Review*, 53, 77–104.

Engels, Frederick 1884/1972: *The Origin of the Family, Private Property and the State*. New York: International Publishers.

Evans, Judith 1986: Feminism and political theory. In Judith Evans et al. *Feminism and Political Theory*, London: Sage, 1–16.

Feldberg, Roslyn and Glenn, Evelyn Nakano 1984: Male and female: job versus gender models in the sociology of work. In Janet Siltanen and Michele Stanworth (eds), *Women and the Public Sphere*, London: Hutchinson, 23–36.

Felski, Rita 1989a: *Beyond Feminist Aesthetics*. Cambridge, MA: Harvard University Press.

——1989b: Feminist theory and social change. *Theory, Culture and Society*, 6, 219–40.

——1989c: Feminism, postmodernism, and the critique of modernity. *Cultural Critique*, 13, 33–56.

Ferguson, Kathy 1984: *The Feminist Case against Bureaucracy*. Philadelphia: Temple University Press.

——1993: *The Man Question: Visions of Subjectivity in Feminist Theory*. Berkeley: University of California Press.

Fierlbeck, Katherine 1991: Redefining responsibility: the politics of citizenship in the United Kingdom. *Canadian Journal of Political Science*, XXIV (3), 575–93.

Finch, Janet 1983: *Married to the Job*. London, Sydney and Boston: Allen & Unwin.

Firestone, Shulamith 1970: *The Dialectic of Sex*. New York: Bantam Books.

Flax, Jane 1987: Postmodernism and gender relations in feminist theory. *Signs*, 12 (4), 621–43.

Foucault, Michel 1969/1972: *The Archaeology of Knowledge*, trans A. M. Sheridan-Smith. New York: Harper & Row [orig. pubd as *L'archéologie du savoir*, Paris].

——1976/1978: *The History of Sexuality*, Vol. 1, trans. R. Hurley. New York: Vintage Books [orig. pubd as *La Volente de savoir*, Paris: Gallimard].

——1980: *Power/Knowledge: Selected Interviews and other Writings* (Colin Gordon, ed.). New York: Pantheon.

——1981: The subject and power. *Critical Inquiry*, 8, 777–95.

Fowlkes, Martha 1980: *Behind every Successful Man*, New York: Columbia University Press.

Franzen, Monika and Ethiel, Nancy 1988: *Make Way! 200 Years of American Women in Cartoons*. Chicago: Chicago Review Press.

Fraser, Nancy 1989: *Unruly Practices: Power, Discourse and Gender in Contemporary Social Theory*. Cambridge: Polity Press; Minneapolis: University of Minnesota Press.

——1990: Rethinking the public sphere: a contribution to the critique of actually existing democracy. *Social Text*, 25/26, 56–80.

——1992a: The uses and abuses of French discourse theories for feminist politics. *Theory, Culture and Society*, 9, 51–71.

——1992b: Sex, lies and the public sphere: some reflections on the confirmation of Clarence Thomas. *Critical Inquiry*, 18, 595–612.

Fraser, Nancy and Bartky, Sandra (eds) 1992: *Revaluing French Feminism*. Indianapolis: Indiana University Press.

Fraser, Nancy and Nicholson, Linda 1990: Social criticism without philosophy: an encounter between feminism and postmodernism. In Linda Nicholson (ed.), *Feminism/Postmodernism*. New York: Routledge, 19–38.

Fromm, Erich 1932/1978: The method and function of an analytic social psychology. In A. Arato and E. Gebhardte (eds), *The Essential Frankfurt School Reader*, New York: Urizen Books, 477–96.

Fuss, Diana 1989: *Essentially Speaking: Feminism, Nature and Difference*. New York: Routledge.

Gaffield, Chad 1984: Wage labour, industrialization and the origins of the modern family. In M. Baker (ed.), *The Family: Changing Trends in Canada*, Toronto: McGraw Hill Ryerson, 21–34.

Gane, Mike 1983: Durkheim: woman as outsider. *Economy and Society*, 12, 227–70.

Garmanikow, E. 1978: Sexual division of labour: the case of nursing. In A. Kuhn and A. Wolpe (eds), *Feminism and Materialism*, London: Routledge & Kegan Paul, 96–123.

Garnsey, Elizabeth, Rubery, Jill and Wilkinson, Frank 1985: Labour market structure and work-force divisions. In Rosemary Deem and Graeme Salaman (eds), *Work, Culture and Society*, Milton Keynes: Open University Press, 40–76.

Giddens, Anthony 1971: *Capitalism and Modern Social Theory*. Cambridge: Cambridge University Press.

——1973: *The Class Structure of the Advanced Societies*. London: Hutchinson.

——1976: *The New Rules of Sociological Method*. London: Hutchinson.

——1979: *Central Problems in Social Theory*. London: Macmillan.

——1981: *A Contemporary Critique of Historical Materialism*. Berkeley: University of California Press.

——1984: *The Constitution of Society: Outline of a Theory of Structuration*. Berkeley: University of California Press.

——1987: *Social Theory and Modern Sociology*. Cambridge: Polity Press.

——1989: A reply to my critics. In D. Held and J. Thompson (eds), *Social Theory of Modern Societies: Anthony Giddens and his Critics*, Cambridge: Cambridge University Press, 249–301.

——1990: *The Consequences of Modernity*. Stanford, CA: Stanford University Press.

——1991: *Modernity and Self-Identity*. Cambridge: Polity Press.

Gilligan, Carol 1982: *In a Different Voice*. Cambridge, MA: Harvard University Press.

Giminez, Martha 1982: The oppression of women. In Ino Rossi (ed.), *Structural Sociology*, New York: Columbia University Press, 292–324.

——1987: Marxist and non-Marxist elements in Engels' views on the oppression of women. In Janet Sayers, Mary Evans and Nanneke Redclift (eds), *Engels Revisited: New Feminist Essays*, New York and London: Tavistock, 37–56.

Giroux, Henry 1981: Hegemony, resistance and the paradox of educational reform. *Interchange*, 12 (2/3), 3–26.

——1983a: Rationality, reproduction and resistance. *Current Perspectives in Social Theory*, 4, 85–117.

——1983b: *Theory and Resistance in Education*. South Hadley, MA: Bergin & Garvey.

Glenn, Evelyn Nakano 1991: Racial ethnic women's labour: the intersection of race, gender, and class oppression. In Rae Lesser Blumberg (ed.), *Gender, Family and Economy*, London and Newbury Park, CA: Sage, 173–201.

Goldthorpe, John 1983: Women and class analysis: in defense of the conventional view. *Sociology*, 17 (4), 465–88.

——1984: Women and class analysis: a reply to the replies. *Sociology*, 18 (4), 491–9.

Gordon, Linda 1986: What's new in women's history. In Teresa de Lauretis (ed.), *Feminist Studies/Critical Studies*, Bloomington: Indiana University Press, 20–30.

———1990a: The new feminist scholarship on the welfare state. In Linda Gordon (ed.), *Women, the State and Welfare*, Madison: University of Wisconsin Press, 9–35.

———1990b: The welfare state: towards a socialist-feminist perspective. In Ralph Miliband and Leo Panitch (eds), *The Socialist Register* 1990, London: Merlin Press, 171–200.

Gouldner, Alvin 1983: *The Two Marxisms*. New York: Seabury.

Graham, Hilary 1983: Caring: a labour of love. In J. Finch and D. Groves (eds), *Labour of Love: Women, Work and Caring*, London: Routledge & Kegan Paul, 13–30.

Gramsci, Antonio 1929–35/1971: *Selections from the Prison Notebooks*, ed. and trans. Q. Hoare and G. Nowell Smith. New York: International Publishers; London: Lawrence & Wishart.

Greico, M. and Whipp, R. 1986: Women and the workplace: gender and control in the labour process. In D. Knights and H. Wilmott (eds), *Gender and the Labour Process*, Brookfield, VT: Gower, 117–39.

Guess, Raymond 1981: *The Idea of a Critical Theory*. Cambridge: Cambridge University Press.

Habermas, Jürgen 1968/1971: *Knowledge and Human Interests*, trans. J. Shapiro. Boston: Beacon Press [orig. pubd as *Erkenntnis und Interesse*, Frankfurt am Main: Suhrkamp].

———1971/1974: *Theory and Practice*, trans. J. Viertel. London: Heinemann [orig. pubd as *Theorie und Praxis*, Frankfurt am Main: Suhrkamp].

———1973/1975: *Legitimation Crisis*, trans. T. McCarthy. Boston: Beacon Press [orig. pubd as *Legitimations-probleme in Spätkapitalismus*, Frankfurt am Main: Suhrkamp].

———1976/1979: *Communication and the Evolution of Society*, trans. T. McCarthy. Boston: Beacon Press [orig. pubd as *Sprachpragmatik und Philosophie/Zur Rekonstruktion des Historischen Materialismus*, Frankfurt am Main: Suhrkamp].

———1981: Modernity versus postmodernity. *New German Critique*, 22, 3–14.

———1982: Reply to my critics. In J. Thompson and D. Held (eds), *Habermas: Critical Debates*, Cambridge, MA: MIT Press, 219–83.

———1981/1984: *The Theory of Communicative Action*, vol. 1: *Reason and the Rationalization of Society*, trans. T. McCarthy. Boston: Beacon Press [orig. pubd as *Theorie des Kommunikativen Handelns*, vol. 1, Frankfurt am Main: Suhrkamp].

———1986: *Autonomy and Solidarity*, ed. Peter Dews. London: Verso.

———1981/1987a: *The Theory of Communicative Action*, vol. 2: *Lifeworld and*

System, trans. T. McCarthy. Boston: Beacon Press [orig. pubd as *Theorie des Kommunikativen Handelns*, vol. 2, Frankfurt am Main: Suhrkamp].

——1985/1987b: *The Philosophical Discourse of Modernity*, trans. F. Lawrence. Cambridge, MA: MIT Press [orig. pubd as *Der philosophische Diskurs der Moderne*, Frankfurt am Main: Surhkamp].

——1985/1989a: *The New Conservatism*, ed. and trans. Shierry Weber Nicholsen. Cambridge, MA: MIT Press.

——1962/1989b: *The Structural Transformation of the Public Sphere*, trans. T. Burger. Cambridge, MA: MIT Press [orig. pubd as *Strukfurwandel der Offentlichheit*, Darmstadt: Hermann Luchterhand].

——1992: Further reflections on the public sphere. In Craig Calhoun (ed.), *Habermas and the Public Sphere*, Cambridge, MA: MIT Press, 421–61.

Hacker, Sally 1989: *Pleasure, Power and Technology*. Boston: Unwin Hyman.

Hakim, Catherine 1988: Homeworking in Britain. In R. A. Pahl (ed.), *On Work: Historical, Comparative and Theoretical Perspectives*, Oxford: Blackwell, 609–32.

Hall, Stuart 1980: 'Cultural studies': two paradigms. *Media, Culture and Society*, 2, 57–72.

——1981: In defense of theory. In R. Samuel (ed.), *People's History and Socialist Theory*, London: Routledge & Kegan Paul, 378–85.

——1988: The toad in the garden: Thatcherism among the theorists. In Cary Nelson and Lawrence Grossberg (eds), *Marxism and the Interpretation of Culture*, Chicago, University of Illinois Press, 35–73.

Hall, Stuart and Jefferson, T. 1976: *Resistance through Ritual*. London: Hutchinson.

Hansen, Karen V. and Philipson, Ilene J. (eds) 1990: *Women, Class and the Feminist Imagination*. Philadelphia: Temple University Press.

Harding, Sandra 1986: *The Science Question in Feminism*. Ithaca, NY: Cornell University Press.

Harris, C. C. 1983: *The Family and Industrial Society*. London, Sydney and Boston: George Allen & Unwin.

Hartmann, Heidi 1979: Capitalism, patriarchy and job segregation by sex. In Zillah Eisenstein (ed.), *Capitalist Patriarchy and the Case for Socialist Feminism*, New York: Monthly Review Press, 206–47.

——1981: The unhappy marriage of Marxism and feminism: towards a more progressive union. In L. Sargent (ed.), *Women and Revolution: The Unhappy Marriage of Marxism and Feminism*, Boston: South End Press, 1–42.

Hartsock, Nancy 1985: *Money, Sex and Power*. Boston: Northeastern University Press.

——1987: Rethinking modernism: minority vs. majority theories. *Cultural Critique*, 7, 187–206.

——1989: Postmodernism and political change: issues for feminist theory. *Cultural Critique*, 14, 15–33.

Hawkesworth, Mary E. 1989: Knowers, knowing, known: feminist theory and claims of truth. *Signs*, 14 (3), 533–57.

Heath, Anthony and Britten, Nicky 1984: Women's jobs do make a difference: a reply to Goldthorpe. *Sociology*, 18 (4), 475–90.

Hegel, G. W. F. 1821/1967: *Philosophy of Right*. Oxford: Oxford University Press.

Held, David 1980: *Introduction to Critical Theory*. London, Hutchinson; Berkeley: University of California Press.

Held, David and Thompson, John (eds) 1989: *Social Theory of Modern Societies: Anthony Giddens and his Critics*. Cambridge: Cambridge University Press.

Hennessy, Rosemary 1993: *Materialist Feminism and the Politics of Discourse*. New York: Routledge.

Henriques, J., Hollway, W., Unwin, C., Venn, C. and Walkerdine, V. 1984: *Changing the Subject: Psychology, Social Regulation and Subjectivity*. London: Methuen.

Hochschild, Arlie 1989: *The Second Shift: Working Parents and the Revolution at Home*. New York: Viking Books.

Hohendahl, Peter 1979: Critical theory, public sphere and culture: Jürgen Habermas and his critics. *New German Critique*, 16, 89–118.

hooks, bell 1990: *Yearnings: Race, Gender and Cultural Politics*. Toronto: Between the Lines.

——1991: Sisterhood: political solidarity between women. In Sneja Gunew (ed.) *A Reader in Feminist Knowledge*, London: Routledge, 27–41.

Horkheimer, Max 1972: *Critical Theory*. New York: Seabury Press.

Howard, Dick 1977: *The Marxian Legacy*. New York: Urizen Books.

Humphries, Jane 1987: The origin of the family: born out of scarcity not wealth. In J. Sayers, M. Evans and N. Redclift (eds), *Engels Revisited: New Feminist Essays*, New York and London: Tavistock, 11–36.

Humphries, Jane and Rubery, Jill 1984: The reconstitution of the supply side of the labour market: the relative autonomy of social reproduction. *Cambridge Journal of Economics*, 8 (4), 331–46.

Irigaray, Luce 1985: *This Sex which is not One*. Ithaca, NY: Cornell University Press.

Jaggar, Alison 1983: *Feminist Politics and Human Nature*. London: Harvester.

Jay, Martin 1984: *Marxism and Totality*. Berkeley: University of California Press.

Jenson, Jane 1986: Gender and reproduction: or, babies and the state. *Studies in Political Economy*, 20, 9–46.

——1987: Changing discourse, changing agendas: political rights and reproductive policies in France. In Mary Fainsod Katzenstein and Carol McClurg Mueller (eds), *The Women's Movements of the United States and Western Europe*, Philadelphia: Temple University Press, 64–88.

——1989: 'Different' but not 'exceptional': Canada's permeable Fordism. *Canadian Review of Sociology and Anthropology*, 26 (1), 69–94.

——1990: Representations of difference: the varieties of French feminism. *New Left Review*, 180, 127–60.

Jessop, Bob 1982: *The Capitalist State*. New York: New York University Press.

Kamenka, Eugene 1983: Marxism and the public/private distinction. In S. I. Benn and G. F. Gaus (eds), *Public and Private in Social Life*. New York: St Martin's Press, 267–79.

Kandal, Terry K. 1988: *The Woman Question in Classical Social Theory*. Miami: Florida International University Press.

Kanter, Rosabeth Moss 1977: *Men and Women of the Corporation*. New York: Basic Books.

Katz, Michael B. 1982: *The Social Organization of Early Industrial Capitalism*. Cambridge, MA: Harvard University Press.

Keane, John 1984: *Public Life and Late Capitalism: Towards a Socialist Theory of Democracy*. Cambridge: Cambridge University Press.

——1988: Introduction. In John Keane (ed.), *Civil Society and the State*, London: Verso, 1–31.

Kellner, Douglas 1989: *Critical Theory, Marxism and Modernity*. Cambridge: Polity Press; Baltimore: Johns Hopkins University Press.

——1990: The postmodern turn: positions, problems and prospects. In George Ritzer (ed.), *Frontiers of Social Theory: The New Syntheses*, New York: Columbia University Press, 255–86.

Kessler-Harris, Alice 1988: The just price, the free market and the value of women. *Feminist Studies*, 14 (2), 235–49.

Kinsman, Gary 1987: *The Regulation of Desire*. Montreal: Black Rose Books.

Kirk, Sylvia van 1986: The role of native women in the fur trade society of Western Canada, 1670–1830. In V. Strong-Boag and A. Fellman (eds), *Rethinking Canada: The Promise of Women's History*, Toronto: Copp Clark Pitman, 59–66.

Koven, Seth and Michel, Sonya 1990: Womanly duties: maternalist politics and the origins of welfare states in France, Germany, Great

Britain and the United States, 1880–1920. *American Historical Review*, 95(4), 1076–108.

Kristeva, Julia 1980: *Desire in Language*. New York: Columbia University Press.

——1981: Woman can never be defined. In Elaine Marks and Isabelle de Courtivron (eds). *New French Feminisms: An Anthology*, New York: Schocken, 137–41.

——1982: Women's time. In Nannerl O. Keohane, Michelle Z. Rosaldo and Barbara C. Gelpi (eds), *Feminist Theory: A Critique of Ideology*. Chicago: University of Chicago Press, 31–53.

Laclau, Ernesto and Mouffe, Chantal 1985: *Hegemony and Socialist Strategy*. London: Verso.

Landes, Joan 1984: Women and the public sphere: a modern perspective. *Social Analysis*, 15, 20–31.

——1988: *Women and the Public Sphere in the Age of the French Revolution*. Ithaca, NY: Cornell University Press.

Lasch, Christopher 1979: *Haven in a Heartless World*. New York: Basic Books.

Laslett, Peter and Wall, Richard (eds) 1972: *Household and Family in Past Time*. Cambridge: Cambridge University Press.

Lawrence, Philip K. 1989: The state and legitimation: the work of Jürgen Habermas. In Graeme Duncan (ed.), *Democracy and the Capitalist State*, Cambridge: Cambridge University Press, 133–58.

Leonard, Stephen 1990: *Critical Theory in Political Practice*. Princeton, NJ: Princeton University Press.

Lerner, Gerda 1986: *The Creation of Patriarchy*. New York: Oxford University Press.

Levine, David 1989: Recombinant family formation strategies. *Journal of Historical Sociology*, 2 (2), 89–115.

Lewis, Debra 1988: *Just Give us the Money*. Vancouver: Women's Research Centre.

Lewis, Jane 1985: The debate on sex and class. *New Left Review*, 149, 108–20.

——1986: The working-class wife and mother and state intervention, 1870–1918. In Jane Lewis (ed.), *Labour and Love: Women's Experience of Home and Family, 1850–1940*, Oxford: Blackwell, 99–120.

Lieven, Elena 1981: Subjectivity, materialism and patriarchy. In Cambridge Women's Studies Group (ed.), *Women in Society*, London: Virago, 257–75.

Livesay, Jeff 1985: Normative grounding and praxis: Habermas, Giddens and a contradiction within critical theory. *Sociological Theory*, 3, 66–76.

Lowe, Graham 1987: *Women in the Administrative Revolution*. Toronto: University of Toronto Press.

Lown, J. 1983: Not so much a factory as a form of patriarchy. In E. Garmanikow, D. Morgan, J. Purvis and D. Taylorson (eds), *Gender, Class and Work*, London: Heinemann, 28–45.

Luxton, Meg 1980: *More than a Labour of Love: Three Generations of Women's Work in the Home*. Toronto: Women's Press.

———1987: Thinking about the future. In Karen Anderson (ed.), *Family Matters*, Toronto: Methuen, 237–60.

———1990: Two hands for the clock: changing patterns in the gendered division of labour in the home. In Sedef Arat-Koç, Meg Luxton and Harriet Rosenberg (eds), *Through the Kitchen Window: The Politics of Home and Family* (2nd, enlarged edn), Toronto: Garamond, 39–55.

Lyotard, Jean-François 1984: *The Postmodern Condition*. Minneapolis: University of Minnesota Press.

MacDonald, Eleanor 1991: The trouble with subjects: feminism, Marxism and the questions of poststructuralism. *Studies in Political Economy*, 35, 43–71.

Macfarlane, Alan 1978: *The origins of English Individualism*. Oxford: Blackwell.

McIntosh, Mary 1978: The state and the oppression of women. In Annette Kuhn and Ann Marie Wolpe (eds), *Feminism and Materialism*, London: Routledge & Kegan Paul, 254–89.

MacKinnon, Catharine A. 1982: Feminism, Marxism, method and the state. In N. O. Keohane, M. Z. Rosaldo and B. C. Gelpi (eds), *Feminist Theory: A Critique of Ideology*, Chicago: University of Chicago Press, 1–30.

———1989: *Towards a Feminist Theory of the State*. Cambridge, MA: Harvard University Press.

Mackintosh, M. 1981: Gender and economics: the sexual division of labour and the subordination of women. In Kate Young, Carol Wolkowitz and Roslyn McCullogh (eds), *Of Marriage and the Market*, London: CSE Books, 1–15.

Mandell, Nancy 1988: The child question: links between women and children in the family. In N. Mandell and A. Duffy (eds), *Reconstructing the Canadian Family*, Toronto: Butterworths, 49–81.

Mann, Michael 1986: A crisis in stratification theory? In Rosemary Crompton and Michael Mann (eds), *Gender and Stratification*, Cambridge: Polity Press, 40–56.

Marsden, Lorna 1981: The 'labour force' is an ideological structure: a guiding note to the labour economists. *Atlantis*, 7 (1), 57–64.

Marshall, Barbara L. 1988: Feminist theory and critical theory. *Canadian Review of Sociology and Anthropology*, 25 (2), 208–30.

——1991: Re-producing the gendered subject. *Current Perspectives in Social Theory*, 11, 169–95.

Marshall, T. H. 1950: *Citizenship and Social Class*. Cambridge: Cambridge University Press.

Martin, Biddy 1988: Feminism, criticism and Foucault. In Irene Diamond and Lee Quinby (eds), *Feminism and Foucault: Reflections on Resistance*, Boston: Northeastern University Press, 3–19.

Marx, Karl 1867/1946: *Capital*, Vol. 1, trans. S. Moore and E. Aveling. London: Allen & Unwin.

——1847/1963: *The Poverty of Philosophy*. New York: International Publishers [orig. pubd as *Misère de la philosophie*, Paris: A. Frank].

——1857–8/1973: *Grundrisse*, trans. M. Nicolaus. London: Pelican.

Marx, Karl and Engels, Frederick 1848/1948: *The Communist Manifesto*. New York: International Publishers.

——1845–6/1970: *The German Ideology*. New York: International Publishers.

Matthews, Jill Julius 1984: *Good and Mad Women*. London, Sydney and Boston: George Allen & Unwin.

Middleton, Chris 1974: Sexual inequality and stratification theory. In Frank Parkin (ed.) *The Social Analysis of Class Structure*, New York and London: Tavistock, 179–203.

Milkman, Ruth 1983: Female factory labour and industrial structure. *Politics and Society*, 12 (2), 159–203.

Miliband, Ralph 1969: *The State in Capitalist Society*. London: Weidenfeld & Nicolson.

Mills, Patricia J. 1987: *Woman, Nature and Psyche*. New Haven, CT: Yale University Press.

Mitchell, Juliet 1971: *Women's Estate*. New York: Vintage Books.

——1974: *Psychoanalysis and Feminism*. New York: Vintage Books.

Mitter, Swasti 1986: *Common Fate, Common Bond: Women in the Global Economy*. London: Pluto.

Modleski, Tania 1991: *Feminism without Women*. London: Routledge.

Mohanty, Chandra Talpade 1991: Cartographies of struggle: third-world women and the politics of feminism. In Chandra Talpade Mohanty, Ann Russo and Lourdes Torres (eds), *Third World Women and the Politics of Feminism*, Bloomington: Indiana University Press, 1–47.

Moraga, C. and Anzaldua, G. (eds) 1983: *This Bridge Called my Back: Writings by Radical Women of Colour*. New York: Kitchen Table/Women of Color Press.

Morgan, D. H. J. 1985: *The Family, Politics and Social Theory*. London: Routledge & Kegan Paul.

Morgen, Sandra 1990: Conceptualizing and changing consciousness: socialist feminist perspectives. In K. Hansen and Ilene J. Philipson (eds), *Women, Class and the Feminist Imagination*, Philadelphia: Temple University Press, 277–91.

Morrow, Raymond A. 1985: Critical theory and critical sociology. *Canadian Review of Sociology and Anthropology*, 22 (5), 710–47.

——1988: The developmental subject: Habermas and the reproduction of the lifeworld. Unpublished paper, presented to the Multidisciplinary Conference on Rethinking the Subject in Discourse, McGill University, Montreal, 18–20 March 1988.

——1991: Critical theory, Gramsci and cultural studies: from structuralism to poststructuralism. In Philip Wexler (ed.), *Critical Theory Now*, London: Falmer Press, 27–70.

Morrow, Raymond and Torres, Carlos 1987: Social theory, social reproduction and education's everyday life. Unpublished paper, presented to the Western Association of Sociology and Anthropology Association Annual Meeting, Edmonton, Alberta, 18–29 February, 1987.

Murgatroyd, Linda 1989: Only half the story: some blinkering effects of 'malestream' sociology. In D. Held and J. Thompson (eds), *Social Theory of Modern Societies: Anthony Giddens and his Critics*, Cambridge: Cambridge University Press, 147–61.

Nett, Emily 1981: Canadian families in socio-historical perspective. *Canadian Journal of Sociology*, 6 (3), 239–60.

Ng, Roxana 1988: *The Politics of Community Services: Immigrant Women, Class and the State*. Toronto: Garamond.

Nicholson, Linda 1986: *Gender and History: The Limits of Social Theory in the Age of the Family*. New York: Columbia University Press.

——1987: Feminism and Marx: integrating kinship with the economic. In Seyla Benhabib and Drucilla Cornell (eds), *Feminism as Critique*, Oxford: Blackwell; Minneapolis: University of Minnesota Press, 16–30.

——(ed.) 1990: *Feminism/Postmodernism*. New York: Routledge.

——1992: On the postmodern barricades: feminism. In Steven Seidman and David Wagner (eds), *Postmodernism and Social Theory*, Oxford: Blackwell, 82–100.

O'Brien, Mary 1981: *The Politics of Reproduction*. London: Routledge & Kegan Paul.

——1984: Hegemony and superstructure. In Jill McCalla Vickers (ed.), *Taking Sex into Account*, Ottawa: Carleton University Press, 85–100.

OECD 1985: *The Integration of Women into the Economy*. Paris: Organization for Economic Cooperation and Development.

Offe, Claus 1984: *Contradictions of the Welfare State*. Cambridge, MA: MIT Press.

——1985: New social movements: challenging the boundaries of institutional politics. *Social Research*, 52 (4), 817–68.

Omvedt, Gail 1986: Patriarchy: the analysis of women's oppression. *The Insurgent Sociologist*, 13 (3), 30–50.

Ortner, Sherry 1974: Is female to male as nature is to culture? In Michele Zimbalist Rosaldo and Louise Lamphere (eds), *Women, Culture and Society*, Stanford, CA: Stanford University Press, 43–87.

Pahl, R. E. 1984: *Divisions of Labour*. Oxford: Blackwell.

Papanek, Hanna 1973: Men, women and work: reflections on the two-person career. *American Journal of Sociology*, 78 (4), 852–72.

Parsons, Talcott and Bales, Robert 1955: *Family: Socialization and Interaction Process*. New York: Free Press.

Pateman, Carole 1988: *The Sexual Contract*. Stanford, CA: Stanford University Press.

Pearson, Ruth 1988: Female workers in the first and third worlds: the greening of women's labour. In R. A. Pahl (ed.), *On Work: Historical, Comparative and Theoretical Approaches*, Oxford: Blackwell, 449–66.

Phillips, Anne and Taylor, Barbara 1986: Sex and skill. In Feminist Review (ed.), *Waged Work: A Reader*, London: Virago, 54–66.

Pierson, Christopher 1984: New theories of state and civil society: recent developments in post-Marxist analyses of the state. *Sociology*, 18 (4): 562–71.

Pierson, Ruth Roach 1983: *Canadian Women and the Second World War*. Canadian Historical Association: Booklet 37.

Poggi, Gianfranco 1990: Anthony Giddens and 'the Classics'. In J. Clark, C. Modgil and F. Modgil (eds), *Anthony Giddens: Consensus and Controversy*, London: Falmer Press, 11–19.

Porter, Marilyn 1985: She was skipper of a shore crew: notes on the history of the sexual division of labour in Newfoundland. *Labour/Le Travail*, 15, 105–23.

Poster, Mark 1984: *Foucault, Marxism and History*. Cambridge: Polity Press.

——1989: *Critical Theory and Poststructuralism: In Search of a Context*. Ithaca, NY: Cornell University Press.

Poulantzas, Nicos 1978: *State, Power, Socialism*. London: New Left Books.

Prentice, Alison 1977: The feminization of teaching. In Alison Prentice and Susan Mann Trofimenkoff (eds), *The Neglected Majority*, Toronto: McClelland & Stewart, 49–65.

Prentice, Alison, Bourne, Paula, Brandt, Gail Cuthbert, Light, Beth, Mitchison, Wendy, and Black, Naomi (eds) 1988: *Canadian Women: A History*. Toronto: Harcourt Brace Jovanovich.

Rabine, Leslie 1988: A feminist politics of non-identity. *Feminist Studies*, 14 (1), 11–31.

Ramazanoglu, Caroline 1989: *Feminism and the Contradictions of Oppression*. London: Routledge.

Randall, Melanie 1988: Feminism and the state: questions for theory and practice. *Resources for Feminist Research*, 17 (3), 10–17.

Rapp, Rayna 1979: Household and family. *Feminist Studies*, 5 (1), 175–81.

——1982: Family and class in contemporary America: notes toward an understanding of ideology. In B. Thorne and M. Yalom (eds), *Rethinking the Family*, New York: Longman, 168–87.

Redclift, Nanneke 1988: Gender, accumulation and the labour process. In R. A. Pahl (ed.), *On Work: Historical, Comparative and Theoretical Perspectives*, Oxford: Blackwell, 428–48.

Redclift, Nanneke and Mingione, Enzo (eds) 1985: *Beyond Employment: Household, Gender and Subsistence*. Oxford: Blackwell.

Rich, Adrienne 1977: *Of Women Born*. Toronto: Bantam Books.

Riley, Denise 1983: *War in the Nursery: Theories of the Child and Mother*. London: Virago.

——1988: *Am I That Name? Feminism and the Category of 'Woman' in History*. Minneapolis: University of Minnesota Press.

Rorty, Richard 1979: *Philosophy and the Mirror of Nature*. Princeton, NJ: Princeton University Press.

Rosaldo, Michele Zimbalist 1974: Women, culture and society: a theoretical overview. In Michele Zimbalist Rosaldo and Louise Lamphere (eds), *Women, Culture and Society*, Stanford, CA: Stanford University Press, 17–42.

——1980: The use and abuse of anthropology: reflections on feminism and cross-cultural understanding. *Signs*, 5 (3), 389–417.

Ross, David P. 1990: *Economic Dimensions of Volunteer Work in Canada*. Ottawa: Secretary of State.

Roth, Guenther 1989–90: Durkheim and the principles of 1789: the issue of gender equality. *Telos*, 82, 71–88.

Rothenberg, Paula 1990: The construction, deconstruction and reconstruction of difference. *Hypatia*, 5 (1), 42–57.

Rubery, Jill (ed.) 1988: *Women and Recession*. London: Routledge & Kegan Paul.

Rundell, John F. 1987: *Origins of Modernity*. Cambridge: Polity Press.

Samuelson, Leslie and Marshall, Barbara 1991: The Canadian criminal justice system: inequalities of class, race and gender. In B. Singh Bolaria (ed.), *Issues and Contradictions in Canadian Society*, Toronto: Harcourt Brace Jovanovich, 421–47.

Sargent, Lynda (ed.) 1981: *Women and Revolution: The Unhappy Marriage of Marxism and Feminism*. Boston: South End Press.

Sawicki, Jana 1992: *Disciplining Foucault*. London: Routledge.

Sayer, Derek 1987: *The Violence of Abstraction*. Oxford: Blackwell.

——1991: *Capitalism and Modernity*. New York: Routledge.

Scott, Alison MacEwan 1986: Industrialization, gender segregation and stratification theory. In R. Crompton and M. Mann (eds), *Gender and Stratification*, Cambridge: Polity Press, 154–89.

Scott, Joan 1986: Gender: a useful category of historical analysis. *American Historical Review*, 91 (5), 1053–75.

——1988: *Gender and the Politics of History*. New York: Columbia University Press.

Seidman, Steven 1983: *Liberalism and the Origins of European Social Theory*. Berkeley: University of California Press.

——1991: The end of sociological theory: the postmodern hope. *Sociological Theory*, 9 (2), 131–45.

——1992: Postmodern social theory as narrative with a moral intent. In Steven Seidman and David Wagner (eds), *Postmodernism and Social Theory*, Oxford: Blackwell, 47–81.

Sherover-Marcuse, Erica 1986: *Emancipation and Consciousness*. Oxford: Blackwell.

Smart, Barry 1983: *Foucault, Marxism and Critique*. London: Routledge & Kegan Paul.

——1990: On the disorder of things: sociology, postmodernity and the 'end of the social'. *Sociology*, 24 (3), 397–416.

——1992: *Modern Conditions, Postmodern Controversies*. London: Routledge.

Smith, Dorothy 1974: Women's perspective as a radical critique of sociology. *Sociological Inquiry*, 44, 7–13.

——1985: Women, class and family. In Varda Burstyn and Dorothy Smith, *Women, Class, Family and the State*, Toronto: Garamond, 1–44.

——1987: *The Everyday World as Problematic*. Toronto: University of Toronto Press.

Smith, Pamela 1987: What lies within and behind the statistics? Trying to measure women's contributions to Canadian agriculture. In *Women in Agriculture*, Ottawa: Canadian Advisory Council on the Status of Women, 123–207.

Smith, Paul 1988: *Discerning the Subject*. Minneapolis: University of Minnesota Press.

Sokoloff, Natalie J. 1980: *Between Money and Love: The Dialectics of Women's Home and Market Work*. New York: Praeger.

Soper, Kate 1986: *Humanism and Anti-Humanism*. London: Hutchinson.

——1990: *Troubled Pleasures: Writings on Politics, Gender and Hedonism*. London: Verso.

Spelman, Elizabeth 1988: *Inessential Woman: Problems of Exclusion in Feminist Thought*. Boston: Beacon Press.

Spivak, Gayatri 1987: *In other Worlds: Essays in Cultural Politics*. New York: Methuen.

Stanley, Liz and Wise, Sue 1990: Method, methodology and epistemology in feminist research practices. In Liz Stanley (ed.), *Feminist Praxis*, London: Routledge, 20–60.

Stanworth, Michele 1984: Women and class analysis: a reply to John Goldthorpe. *Sociology*, 18 (2), 159–70.

Stephano, Christine Di 1990: Dilemmas of difference: feminism, modernity and postmodernism. In Linda Nicholson (ed.), *Feminism/Postmodernism*, New York: Routledge, 63–82.

Stone, Lawrence 1977: *The Family, Sex and Marriage in England 1500–1800*. London: Weidenfeld & Nicolson.

Strong-Boag, Veronica 1988: *The New Day Recalled: Lives of Girls and Women in English Canada, 1919–1939*. Markham: Penguin Books.

Sundberg, Sara Brooks 1986: Farm women on the Canadian prairie frontier: the helpmate image. In V. Strong-Boag and A. Fellman (eds), *Rethinking Canada: The Promise of Women's History*, Toronto: Copp Clark Pitman, 95–106.

Sydie, R. A. 1987: *Natural Women, Cultured Men: A Feminist Perspective on Sociological Theory*. Milton Keynes: Open University Press; Toronto: Methuen.

Thomas, Robert J. 1982: Citizenship and gender in work organizations: some considerations for theories of the labour process. In M. Burawoy and T. Skocpol (eds), *Marxist Inquiries: Studies of Labour, Class and States*, supplement to the *American Journal of Sociology*, Chicago: University of Chicago Press, 88, S86–S112.

Thomas, J. J. R. 1985: Rationalization and the status of gender divisions. *Sociology*, 19 (3), 409–20.

Thompson, E. P. 1978: *The Poverty of Theory*. London: Merlin; New York: Monthly Review Press.

Thompson, John 1989: The theory of structuration. In David Held and John Thompson (eds), *Social Theory of Modern Societies: Anthony Giddens and his Critics*. Cambridge: Cambridge University Press, 56–76.

Tilly, Louise A. and Scott, Joan W. 1978, 2/1989: *Women, Work and Family*. New York: Routledge.

Tucker, Robert C. (ed.) 1972, 2/1978: *The Marx–Engels Reader*. New York: Norton.

Turner, Bryan S. 1987: Marx, Weber and the coherence of capitalism. In Norbert Wiley (ed.), *The Marx–Weber Debate*. London and Newbury Park, CA: Sage, 169–204.

——1990a: Outline of a theory of citizenship. *Sociology*, 24(2), 189–217.

——1990b: Periodization and politics in the postmodern. In Bryan S. Turner (ed.), *Theories of Modernity and Postmodernity*, London and Newbury Park, CA: Sage, 1–13.

——1992: Ideology and utopia in the formation of an intelligentsia: reflections on the English cultural conduit. *Theory, Culture and Society*, 9, 183–210.

Ungerson, Clare 1983: Women and caring: skills, tasks and taboos. In E. Garmanikow, D. Morgan, J. Purvis and D. Taylorson (eds), *The Public and the Private*, London: Heinemann, 62–77.

Ursel, Jane 1986: The state and the maintenance of patriarchy. In J. Dickinson and B. Russell (eds), *Family, Economy and State: The Social Reproduction Process under Capitalism*, Toronto: Garamond, 150–191.

Valverde, Mariana 1985: *Sex, Power and Pleasure*. Toronto: Women's Press.

——1991: *The Age of Light, Soap and Water: Moral Reform in English Canada, 1885–1925*. Toronto: McClelland & Stewart.

Valverde, Mariana and Weir, Lorna 1988: The struggles of the immoral: preliminary remarks on moral regulation. *Resources for Feminist Research*, 17 (3), 31–4.

Vellekoop-Baldock, Cora 1990: *Volunteers in Welfare*. London, Sydney and Boston: Allen & Unwin.

Vickers, Jill McCalla 1987: At his mother's knee: sex/gender and the construction of national identities. In Greta Hofmann-Nemiroff (ed.), *Women and Men: Interdisciplinary Readings on Gender*, Toronto: Fitzhenry & Whiteside, 493–514.

Vucht Tijssen, Lieteke van 1990: Women between modernity and postmodernity. In Bryan S. Turner (ed.), *Theories of Modernity and Postmodernity*, London and Newbury Park, CA: Sage, 147–63.

Waerness, Kari 1984: Caring as women's work in the welfare state. In Harriet Holter (ed.), *Patriarchy in a Welfare State*, Oslo: Universitetsforlaget, 67–87.

Walby, Sylvia 1986: *Patriarchy at Work*. Cambridge: Polity Press.

——1990: *Theorizing Patriarchy*. Oxford: Blackwell.

Walker, Pat 1978: Introduction. In Pat Walker (ed.), *Between Labour and Capital*, Montreal: Black Rose Books, xiii–xxx.

Waugh, Patricia 1989: *Feminine Fictions: Revisiting the Postmodern*. London: Routledge.

Weber, Max 1946: *From Max Weber: Essays in Sociology*, ed. H. Gerth and C. W. Mills. New York: Oxford University Press.

——1905/1958: *The Protestant Ethic and the Spirit of Capitalism*, trans. Talcott Parsons. New York: Scribners [orig. pubd as *Die protestantische Ethik und der 'Geist' des Kapitalismus*].

Weedon, Chris 1987: *Feminist Practice and Poststructuralist Theory*. Oxford: Blackwell.

Wellmer, Albrecht 1985: On the dialectic of modernism and post-modernism. *Praxis International*, 4 (4), 337–62.

West, Cornell 1988a: Interview (with Anders Stephenson). In Andrew Ross (ed.), *Universal Abandon? The Politics of Postmodernism*, Minneapolis: University of Minnesota Press, 269–86.

——1988b: Marxist theory and the specificity of Afro-American oppression. In Cary Nelson and Lawrence Grossberg (eds), *Marxism and the Interpretation of Culture*, Chicago: University of Illinois Press, 17–29.

Westwood, S. and Bhachu, P. 1988: *Enterprising Women*. London: Routledge.

Whimster, Sam and Lash, Scott (eds) 1987: *Max Weber, Rationality and Modernity*. London, Sydney and Boston: Allen & Unwin.

Whitebook, Joel 1981: Saving the subject: modernity and the problem of the autonomous individual. *Telos*, 50, 79–103.

——1985: Reason and happiness: some psychoanalytic themes in critical theory. In Richard Bernstein (ed.), *Habermas and Modernity*, Cambridge: Polity Press, 140–60.

Williams, Raymond 1981: *Culture*. Glasgow: Fontana.

Willis, Paul 1981a: *Learning to Labour*. New York: Columbia University Press.

——1981b: Cultural production is different from cultural reproduction is different from social reproduction is different from reproduction. *Interchange*, 12 (2–3), 48–67.

Wilson, Elizabeth 1977: *Women and the Welfare State*. London and New York: Tavistock.

Wilson, Elizabeth (with Angela Weir) 1986: The British Women's Movement. In Elizabeth Wilson, *Hidden Agendas: Theory, Politics and Experience in the British Women's Movement*, London and New York: Tavistock, 93–133.

Yanagisako, Sylvia Junko and Collier, Jane Fishburne 1987: Toward a unified analysis of gender and kinship. In Jane Fishburne Collier and Sylvia Junko Yanagisako (eds), *Gender and Kinship: Essays Toward a Unified Analysis*, Stanford, CA: Stanford University Press, 14–50.

Yeatman, Anna 1986: Women, domestic life and sociology. In C. Pateman and E. Gross (eds), *Feminist Challenges: Social and Political Theory*, London, Sydney and Boston: Allen & Unwin, 157–72.

Young, Iris Marion 1981: Beyond the unhappy marriage: a critique of the dual systems theory. In L. Sargent (ed.), *Women and Revolution: The Unhappy Marriage of Marxism and Feminism*, Boston: South End Press, 43–69.

——1987: Impartiality and the civic public. In Seyla Benhabib and Drucilla Cornell (eds), *Feminism as Critique*, Cambridge: Polity Press; Minneapolis: University of Minnesota Press, 56–79.

Yuval-Davis, Nira 1991: The citizenship debate: women, ethnic processes and the state. *Feminist Review*, 39, 58–67.

Yuval-Davis, Nira and Anthias, Floya 1989: Introduction. In Nira Yuval-Davis and Floya Anthias (eds), *Woman–Nation–State*, London: Macmillan, 1–15.

Index